THIS BOOK IS DEDICATED TO EVERYONE WHO IS TRYING.

A GIFT FOR:

Katherine Elizabeth

FROM:

♡ Mom

Christmas 2017

ACKNOWLEDGMENTS

Special thanks to my parents, Leonard and Kathy Jackson. Their love and support are forever appreciated. Much gratitude to my twin sister Kourtney for always keeping me rooted in the real. Heartfelt appreciation goes out to the friends, family, co-workers, church members, and teachers who encouraged me along the way. Big thanks to my editor, Lindsay Evans, for believing in this project. And, most importantly, thanks to God for being so God.

Copyright © 2015 Hallmark Licensing, LLC

All scripture taken from the HOLY BIBLE: NEW INTERNATIONAL VERSION®. NIV®. Copyright© 1973, 1978, 1984 by International Bible Society. Used by permission of Zondervan.

Published by Hallmark Gift Books, a division of Hallmark Cards, Inc., Kansas City, MO 64141
Visit us on the Web at Hallmark.com.

Editorial Director: Carrie Bolin
Editor: Lindsay Evans
Art Director: Jan Mastin
Designer: Laura Elsenraat
Hand Lettering: Lynn Giunta
Production Designer: Dan Horton

ISBN: 978-1-59530-734-7
BOK2194

Made in China
JUN16

BECAUSE JESUS.

By Keion Jackson

INTRODUCTION

GOD LOVES YOU. PERIOD. This book will try to explain just how much. This book will fail.

This book cannot illustrate the magnitude of God's love because this book is only a book.

And God is much bigger than a book. However, this book will do its best.

The proof that God loves you doesn't lie in the heart, help, and humor found on the following pages.

All of that stuff is just gravy. Here is the meat:

"For God so loved the world that He gave His only begotten Son."

Most people wouldn't give their only begotten french fry, YET GOD GAVE HIS SON.

Quite frankly, that's impressive. Have you ever asked somebody to borrow money and they looked

at you like you were speaking dog? It's like, *"Calm down, dude. I asked for three dollars, not your 401K."*

But God doesn't act like that—HE LOVES; HE GIVES.

AND WHEN GOD GIVES, HE DOESN'T DO IT SHABBY.

God *could* have given us a low-down, dirty son that ate beans and farted all day.

Some disrespectful dude named Sherman that delighted in not leaving a tip for waitresses.

Sherman would have been awful. Sherman would not have died for your sins.

But God did not give us Sherman. He gave us love personified. AND THERE LIES THE PROOF.

How do we know that God cares? BECAUSE JESUS.

How do we know good will ultimately overcome bad? BECAUSE JESUS.

How can we live with hope in our hearts and dancing in our feet, even when times get tough? BECAUSE JESUS.

God's love has many amazing features. It's like a new smart phone, except you won't have to upgrade it every year when a newer version comes out. God's not planning to release the iSalvation 6. HIS LOVE DOESN'T CHANGE. It's constant. And it's for everybody. This book follows suit...
See, this book is for everyone. It's not exclusive, like some trendy nightclub where you have to wear $300 pants to get in.[1] God is not like that. He accepts everybody—even those of us wearing affordable pants.

THIS BOOK IS FOR THE PEOPLE! No matter who you are, or what you've done, GOD HAS LOVE FOR YOU.

Maybe you are very devout. So devout that you named your child Ephesians.[2] On the flipside, maybe faith isn't your thing, and you only pray when you're about to get a speeding ticket. Whatever the case, this book contains spiritual nuggets that your soul might like to taste.

Not only is this book delicious, but it's useful, too! You can pull this puppy out whenever you need a jolt of happiness and inspiration. You can also use it when you need a coaster.
So get ready to read about God's goodness and be reminded that everything will be okay.
Because no weapon formed against us shall prosper.[3]

GOD IS THERE FOR YOU, AND SO IS THIS BOOK. *(But in a much less majestic way.)*

---

[1] If I ever spend $300 on pants, they better be autographed by Christ.

[2] "Whattup. I'm Ephesians, but my friends call me E-Feezy."

[3] Not even bad credit!

WHEN YOU FIRST WAKE UP,
BEFORE YOU BRUSH YOUR TEETH,
you are already loved.

GOD

is THE GOODEST.

SOMETIMES—
YOU JUST GOTTA SIT BACK, RELAX,
AND BEHOLD.

THERE'S NO PANCAKE TOO BIG FOR YOUR HEAVENLY FATHER TO FLIP.

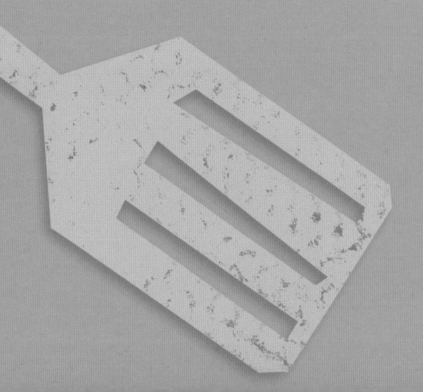

WHEN IT'S HARD TO TRUST IN GOD,

AND YOU'D RATHER DO THINGS YOUR WAY—

IT'S GOOD TO ASK YOURSELF A SIMPLE QUESTION:

"SELF, HOW MANY UNIVERSES HAVE YOU CREATED?"

IF THE ANSWER IS "NO UNIVERSES,"

THEN JUST LET GOD HANDLE THINGS.

GOD'S GOT YOUR BACK.

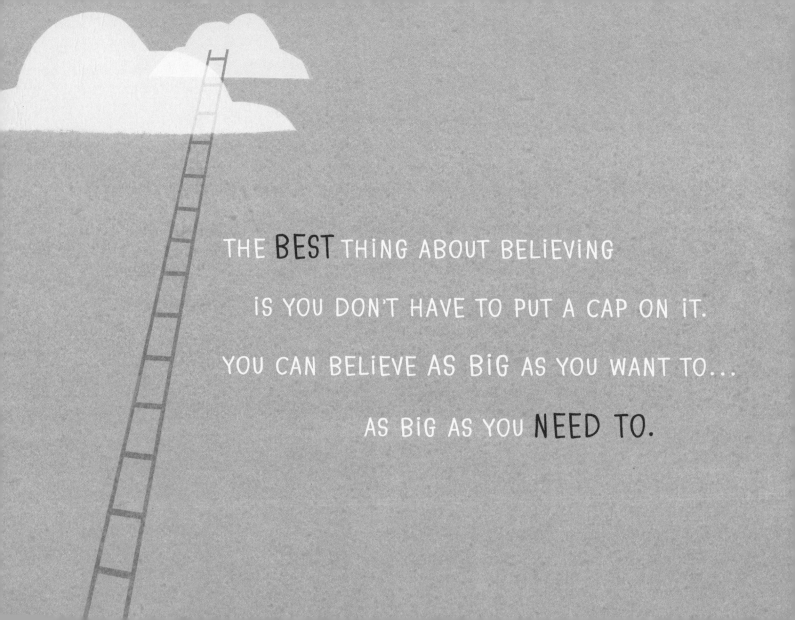

THE **BEST** THING ABOUT BELIEVING

IS YOU DON'T HAVE TO PUT A CAP ON IT.

YOU CAN BELIEVE AS BIG AS YOU WANT TO...

AS BIG AS YOU **NEED TO.**

See—faith is elastic and stretchy.

And no matter what you're going through,

it grows to whatever size we need it to be...

So it's ok to ask for the "IMPOSSIBLE."

Expect the ENORMOUS. Make way for the MIRACULOUS.

Because when God said He could do all things,

He really meant He could do

ALL THINGS.

BEING LOVED BY GOD
IS LIKE WINNING THE LOTTERY

AGAIN AND AGAIN,

OVER AND OVER,

FOREVER AND EVER.

AMEN.

Status Update: BLESSED.

After all these years, God still amazes.

LOVE

is His
DEFAULT
setting.

He did not come to condemn.

One of the many ways God is not like the comment section on YouTube.

Yes, Jesus LOVES me.

(HE LOVES YOU, TOO, BUT WE'RE TALKING ABOUT ME RIGHT NOW.)

SOMETHING MEAN is lurking in the fringes.

It comes to hurt and deceive.

It emerges to smother goodness

and reminds us of when we have fallen short.

"YOU ARE NOT WORTHY," it snivels.

"YOU ARE SMALL, AND YOUR GOD IS WEAK."

It tosses big lies at our feet in hopes that we will stumble.

SOMETHING MEAN is NOT our friend.

BUT DO NOT WORRY.

Because, despite the lurking and loathing,

despite the plotting and the tricks—

even SOMETHING MEAN knows the truth:

We are protected by the love of the ALMIGHTY.

And no matter what... GOD WINS.

Therefore, so do we.

Little stuff.
Big stuff.
Your stuff.
My stuff.

HE'S GOT THE WHOLE WORLD IN HIS HANDS.

GOD'S LOVE IS

ALWAYS
X
NO MATTER WHAT
X
INFINITY
X
FOREVER
+
NOW

Have you ever seen a three-legged dog and thought:

AWW, THAT DOG ONLY HAS THREE LEGS?

The dog is cute, but you feel sorry for it

because it can't catch the squirrel.

And, in a weird way, you like the dog more

BECAUSE iT'S TRYiNG.

THAT'S HOW GOD LOVES US.

He knows we're not perfect,

and we're never gonna catch the squirrel.

But He is GRACiOUS AND MERCiFUL

because three-legged dogs

NEED LOVE, TOO.

HE will
ALWAYS
find something
about us
TO LOVE.

May big, eternal "GOD LOVE" fill your heart right up.

FOR HE
HAS MADE
ice cReam
DELiCiOUS.
LET US RejoiCe
AND BE GLad.

WORRY NOT.
SNACK MUCH.

You and Jesus are on a first-name basis.

How cool is that?

PRAY

WITH EXPECTATION.

If God gave us

E V E R Y T H I N G

we wanted,
we would all have

very junky garages.

"NO"

IS AN ANSWER, TOO, YOU KNOW.

DEAR LORD—

If there's a door
I should not go through,
please CLOSE IT, LOCK IT,
and NAIL IT SHUT.

Please BOARD iT UP,

surround it with BARBED WiRE,

and put a REFRIGERATOR in front of it.

AND A GUARD DOG.
A MEAN one with nothing to lose.

REPENT. REPEAT. REPENT. REPEAT. REPENT. REPEAT. REPENT. REPEAT. REPENT.
REPEAT. REPENT. REPEAT. REPENT. REPEAT. REPENT. REPEAT. REPENT. REPEAT.

GOD SEES THE
BEST IN US AND
FORGIVES
THE REST IN US.

REPENT. REPEAT. REPENT. REPEAT. REPENT. REPEAT. REPENT. REPEAT. REPENT.
REPEAT. REPENT. REPEAT. REPENT. REPEAT. REPENT. REPEAT. REPENT. REPEAT.

HE DOES NOT
KEEP A
"SIN TAB."

I Feel a Hallelujah COMIN' ON!

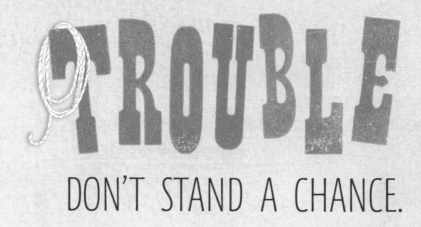

TROUBLE

DON'T STAND A CHANCE.

But thanks be to God! He gives us the victory through our Lord Jesus Christ.
1 Corinthians 15:57 (NIV)

SPOILER ALERT:

GOD WINS

IN THE END.

I CAN'T SAY

you'll never be weary.

I CAN'T SAY

it doesn't get tough.

I CAN'T EVEN SAY

you'll always know where your

next smile is coming from.

BUT WHAT I **CAN** SAY

is that I've tried Jesus,

and HE WORKS.

LORD,
send a revival.

AND LET IT BEGIN WITH MEAT.

LET US GRUB, ONE WITH ANOTHER.

So whether you eat or drink or whatever you do, do it all for the glory of God.

1 Corinthians 10:31 (NIV)

SOMEWHERE,
WAY UP IN THE SKY,

A GOOD THING IS

BEING ASSEMBLED.

Made especially for you.

Every good and perfect gift is from above.
James 1:17 (NIV)

SHUT UP AND TAKE YOUR BLESSING.

LOVE THY CO-WORKER.

Be nice.

JESUS SAiD SO.

Serve one another. *Pie.*

REJOICE.
BE GLAD.
REPEAT.

IT'S NICE TO BE "LIKED." 👍

BUT EVEN BETTER TO BE *loved.*

GOD IS MY BONES.

WITHOUT HIM I CANNOT STAND.

HE IS THE STURDY IN MY FEET

AND THE SOLID IN MY GROUND.

HE STILLS ME WHEN THE WIND WHIPS.

HE STEADIES ME IN THE STORM.

HE IS MY SUPPORT.

HE IS MY FOUNDATION.

HE IS THE REASON I AM STILL HERE.

KNOW GOD.

FEEL LOVE.

NO PUSHiNG, GUYS.

GOD HAS ENOUGH LOVE FOR EVERYBODY.

WHEN GOD SAID
"ALWAYS,"
HE MEANT
"ALWAYS."

GOD WiLL PROViDE.

REFRESHMENTS.

TODAY, I WILL LET God be God.

(Because I suck at it.)

A LITTLE JESUS GOES A LONG WAY.

There will be empty days—hard ones,

when it feels like your heart is runnin' on fumes.

Your body will be a robot, going through the motions—

programmed to simply "get through the day."

There will be times when your head aches

for no apparent reason, and no matter what you do,

you feel a little bit...off.

Unfortunately, those days will happen.

But the good news is GOD has a tomorrow

lined up and Ready to go.

And that's the motivation:

On the other side of a sucky day

is a tomorrow.

PRAISE HIM THROUGH THE SUCKY TIMES.

DARKNESS AIN'T SO TOUGH.

JUST POINT A FLASHLIGHT,

AND IT RUNS AWAY.

CLOUDS COME.

BUT, SO DOES GOD.

BREAKTHROUGHS DON'T HAPPEN OVERNIGHT.

But they happen.

JOY cometh in the morning.

IT'S 6 A.M. SOMEWHERE.

Weeping may stay for the night,
but rejoicing comes in the morning.
Psalm 30:5 (NIV)

Remember that time you were like,

"Oh, no! What am I gonna do?"

But Jesus was like,

"Don't worry—I got this."

…and then everything

turned out all right.

"DONT WORRY—I GOT THIS"

is pretty much the essence of the whole gospel.

It was a dark and spooky night...

THEN JESUS.

The end.

YOU ARE ON

THE RECEIVING END

OF THE

FIERCEST,
MOST POWERFUL LOVE

IN THE UNIVERSE.

REMEMBER:

You are being loved

at every single moment

of every single day.

UP AND DOWN
ALL AROUND—
YOUR LIFE IS TRULY
BLESSED.

Step 1:

REMEMBER YOU WERE

CRAFTED BY GOD.

Step 2:

FEEL BEAUTIFUL.

HE PUT TWINKLE
IN THE STARS.

AND YOU.

It is common for
cracks in courage to occur.

TO REPAIR,

spread a thick coat of spiritual spackle
and wait for substance to dry.

Results WILL NOT vary—

it works EVERY time.

DIFFERENT DAY.
SAME GOD.

TODAY, DISAPPOINT THE DEVIL.

YOU HAVE THE VICTORY!

Behave accordingly.

For God so loved the world
that He gave His one and only Son,
that whoever believes in Him
shall not perish but have eternal life.

John 3:16 (NIV)

YOU ARE SO LOVED.

NEVER FORGET THAT.

Mistake, Schmistake.

THERE'S NEW MERCY FOR EVERY DAY.

STRUGGLE
IS THE
ONLY WAY TO
STRENGTH.

↓

IT'S A

TOUGH WORLD.

STAY

PRAYED UP.

In less than five minutes, I could list a thousand things wrong with me—
from the jacked-up stuff I did last week to the jacked-up stuff
I'm probably gonna do tomorrow. In many ways I am a mess.
Sometimes I want to ask God,

"WHY DO YOU EVEN BOTHER?

WHY NOT QUIT PLAYING, TAKE YOUR BALL, AND GO HOME?

WHY NOT GIVE ME WHAT I DESERVE?

WHY NOT SHOWER ME WITH THE NOTHING I HAVE EARNED?

WHY BLESS? WHY COMFORT? WHY FORGIVE?"

Well, I have come to realize that the answer is very simple: **love.**

HE LOVES
THE STANK
OUT OF YOU.

$$\frac{\text{JESUS} + (\text{ANY SITUATION}) =}{\text{GOING TO BE JUST FINE}}$$

NEVER

UNDERESTIMATE

THE POWER

OF AN

ALL-POWERFUL GOD.

(DUH.)

Guide me, Lord.

Me no know what to do.

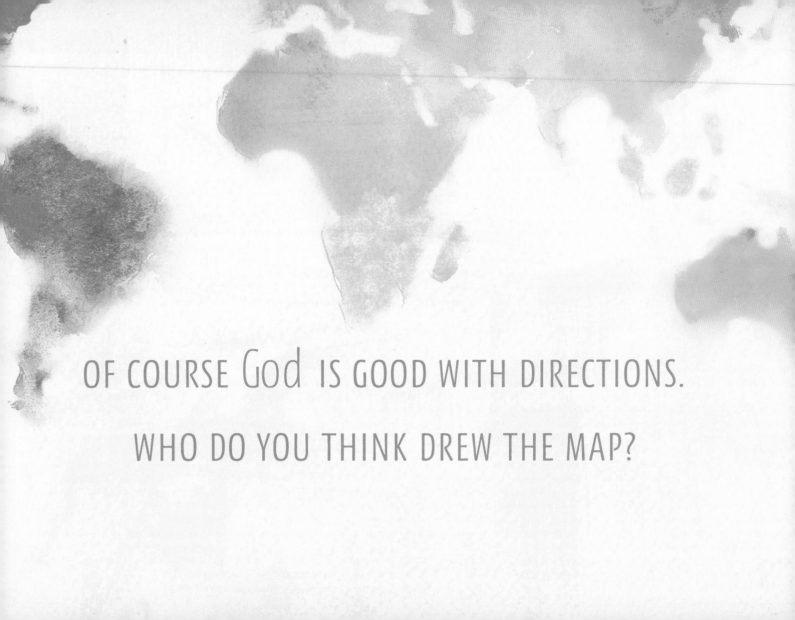

OF COURSE God IS GOOD WITH DIRECTIONS.

WHO DO YOU THINK DREW THE MAP?

FAITH

IS THE ONLY THING BETWEEN HERE AND THERE.

IF YOU'RE GONNA FOLLOW GOD, WEAR COMFORTABLE SHOES.

MISSION: LOVE UNCONDITIONALLY.

BE SOMEBODY'S
BLESSING.

DON'T JUST SIT AROUND—
there is
LOVE
to be
LOVED!

Brethren—
if a neighbor
asks for your last
stick of gum,
SPARE IT.

For his breath may be more stank than yours.

LOVE
LIKE IT'S
THE LAW.
(Because it is.)

ALWAYS
keep a prayer
loaded
and ready to go.

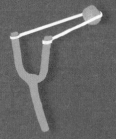

ANGELS

ARE LIKE THE

SECRET SERVICE.

JUST BECAUSE

YOU DON'T SEE THEM

DOESN'T MEAN

THEY'RE NOT AT WORK.

So the Father

hid little, secret blessings along the way.

(Sometimes, in very unusual places!)

For He knew His precious ones

would some days be very tired

and in need of a little comfort.

On a sad and mopey day,

when grayness gathered overhead,

their precious heads hung low.

Then, suddenly. . .

BOOM: a blessing!

Right when they least expected.

And the precious ones continued on, happy.

For the Father knows just what His precious need.

Sometimes nachos

don't have enough cheese.

Which is why

we must be extra thankful

when they do.

i'M NOT SAYiN' iT HELPS

TO END YOUR PRAYERS WiTH

"pretty please,"

BUT i'M NOT SAYiN'

iT DOESN'T HELP, EiTHER.

THE EYES
OF THE LORD
ARE UPON YOU.

(I know. Changes everything, right?)

JESUS,

BE A FENCE AROUND MY

ATTITUDE.

PRAY.
PRAY.
PRAY.

Buy kneepads.

PRAY SOME MORE.

Whether you turn to the right or to the left,

your ears will hear a voice behind you, saying,

"This is the way; walk in it."

Isaiah 30:21 (NIV)

HUSH UP AND LISTEN.

Now is the time to believe—

to lean into HIS LOVE and let your faith happen.

It's the time to look around

and see all the evidence of GOD'S GRACE—

grace that often shows up where it's least expected

and ALWAYS where it's most needed.

If ever there was a time to believe—

in love, in miracles—

it's now.

MAY GOD MOVE
ALL UP & THROUGH
YOUR LIFE.

FAITH-

Just when you think

it's about to throw in the towel...

IT DOESN'T.

BELIEVE
FROM THE GUT.

BE NOT

GRUMPY.

LEAVE ROOM FOR THE HOLY SPIRIT.

AND DESSERT.

YOU'VE GOT A FRIEND IN JESUS.

THE GOOD KIND THAT WON'T ASK YOU TO HELP HiM MOVE.

WITH ARMS OUTSTRETCHED

AND A WARM HUG WAITING,

HE WHISPERS,

"I know. It's OK. Come home."

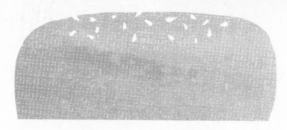

LiFE is A
BLESSiNG
BURGER
WiTH CHEESE.

You are
PERFECTLY,
SPECIFICALLY,
ESPECIALLY
LOVED.

Little pieces of invisible are floating all around you.

They carry wind and breath and words and music.

They lift the sweetest scents up to your nose.

They cool as they zoom by.

They are the atmosphere between us and else,

often mistaken for nothing.

But, my friend, have peace—you are never alone.

For in the little pieces of invisible,

He is present...

HE IS IN THE EVERYWHERE.

If you have enjoyed this book

or it has touched your life in some way,

we would love to hear from you.

Please send your comments to:
Hallmark Book Feedback
P.O. Box 419034
Mail Drop 100
Kansas City, MO 64141

Or e-mail us at:
booknotes@hallmark.com

DEAR GOD:

THANK YOU

INFINITY.

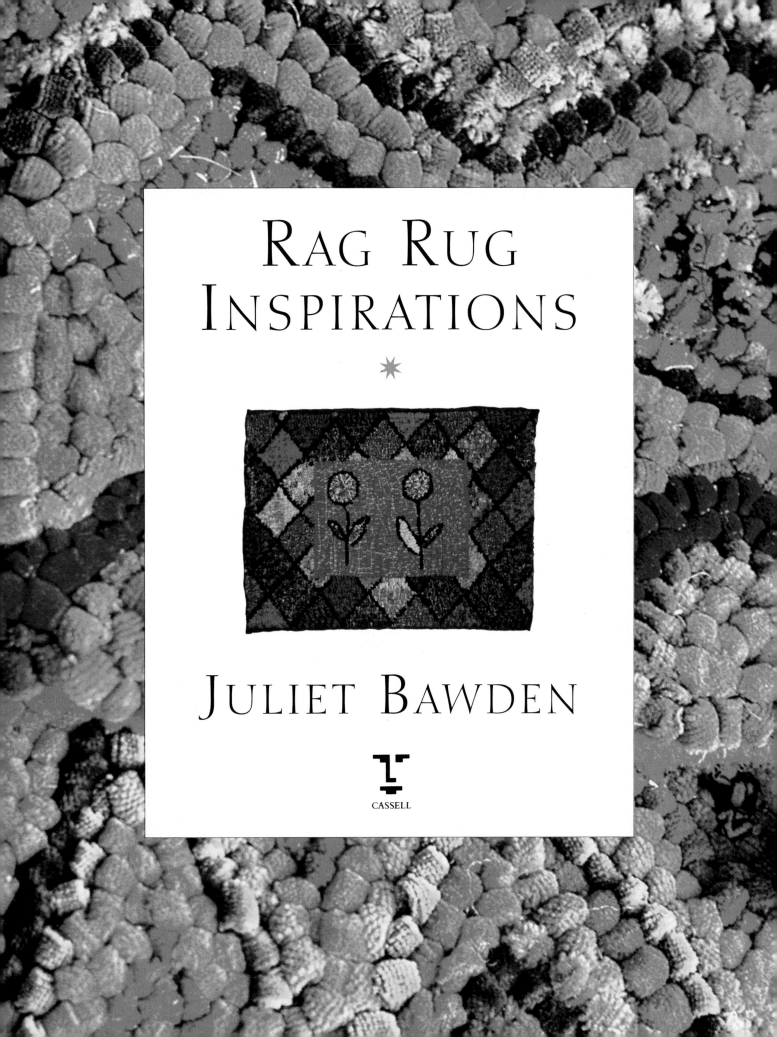

RAG RUG
INSPIRATIONS

✳

JULIET BAWDEN

CASSELL

For Brigette

ACKNOWLEDGEMENTS

✳

I should like to thank Marie-Louise Avery, who took the photographs, and Labeena Ishaque, who styled them. I should also like to acknowledge the help I received from all the rag rug artists who gave so generously of their time and experience. Special thanks to Ann Davies, who is always a fund of information, and to Dee Gilder, whom I met when I had nearly finished the book and who still found new information and new artists.

This edition first published in the UK 1996 by
CASSELL
Wellington House,125 Strand, London, WC2R 0BB

Text copyright © Juliet Bawden 1996
Volume copyright © Cassell 1996

The right of Juliet Bawden to be identified as the author of the work
has been asserted by her in accordance with the Copyright, Designs and Patents Act 1988

Distributed in the United States by
Sterling Publishing Co. Inc.
387 Park Avenue South
New York, NY 10016
USA

Distributed in Australia by
Capricorn Link (Australia) Pty Ltd
2/13 Carrington Road
Castle Hill
NSW 2154

Special photography by Marie-Louise Avery
Photographic styling by Labeena Ishaque
Illustrations by Kate Simunek
Designer Bet Ayer
Editor Lydia Darbyshire

British Library Cataloguing-in-Publication Data
A catalogue record for this book is available from the British Library

ISBN 0 – 304 – 34768 – X

Printed and bound by Bath Press

CONTENTS

✳

Detail of a prodded rug shows how a pattern may be formed through the juxtaposition of rags in different colours and textures.

INTRODUCTION

I have always been fascinated by the idea of making something from scrap materials. I trained as a weaver and then spent a year on a post-graduate course weaving with rags. I was fortunate to have been at Camberwell Art School in London where I was two years below John Hinchcliffe, an innovator in the craft of rag rug making. The book he wrote in 1977, Rugs from Rags, now sadly out of print, is treasured by all those rag rug makers who are lucky enough to possess a copy.

Things have moved on since the 1970s, and rag rug making is enjoying a revival. This is partly no doubt something to do with the political climate of the times and our concerns for the environment, which makes us unhappy about waste. Another reason for the current interest in rag rugs is people's desire to return to their roots and to re-learn some of the old skills. John Hinchcliffe wrote in the introduction to his 1977 book: 'We are now living in a period of re-evaluation, with a practical appreciation of the importance of using our basic resources to the best advantage.' These prophetic words could have been written today.

When I was researching this book I interviewed the designers whose work is featured on the pages that follow, speaking to them in person whenever possible, but otherwise making contact by letter or on the phone. I wanted to know what led them to take up the craft in the first place and also what inspires them to create their designs. Many of them mentioned the freedom of the techniques involved, which do not impose the same restrictions as working with a loom. All the makers and designers I spoke to were generous in discussing their working methods and in passing on their tips and short-cuts, and I hope that you find it as fascinating to read about their work as I did listening to them describe it.

Because the craft of rag rug making has a long history, especially in the United States, Canada and the United Kingdom, the book begins with a brief look at the history of rug making.

I have included 15 different projects in the book, and these use a number of different techniques. When people think of rag rug hooking, mats and wall-hangings usually come to mind, but the hooking technique lends itself to smaller scale pieces, as can be seen in the work of the young British designer Lizzie Reakes, who uses hand hooking to make some modern-looking and unusual jewellery. The projects, therefore, range from small items, such as jewellery, a bag and a hat, to a chair seat and the larger items you would expect to find, such as wall-hangings and, of course, some rugs. Once you have acquired the basic skills, however, you will probably want to experiment and create your own designs for a variety of articles, and I hope that the examples that are illustrated on the pages that follow will encourage and inspire you to try this rewarding and creative craft for yourself.

Juliet Bawden

HISTORY

Although we think of rag rug making as a nineteenth-century phenomenon, there is evidence that the pulled-up weft loop was used as long ago as 2000 BC in Ancient Egypt. The weaving of recycled cloth probably dates from ancient times, too, but the earliest surviving European examples are from the eighteenth century. It is interesting to note that there is also an existing woven rag rug dating from the eighteenth century that was made in Japan, indicating that the technique was used in the Orient.

THE SCANDINAVIAN TRADITION

Sweden and Norway are well known for a particular style of rag weaving known as 'ryer', which involves pulling loops of wool through a woven background to create a fabric that resembled an animal skin. These rugs are first mentioned in inventories and wills dating from about 1700, but fragments of cloth made by this method have been found in Danish bronze age graves. The word 'ryer' or 'ryijs' has been translated as 'rug' or 'rugg', but the fabric made in

Two Northumbrian mat makers using the prodding technique to make a rug on a traditional frame.
The photograph was taken in Hexham in 1875.

Like other Scandinavian countries, Norway has a long tradition of rag rug weaving. Rugs such as these were warm and easily cleaned coverings for the wooden floors.

this way had many more uses than as a floor-covering. The ryer was once used for protection in small, open fishing boats, and by the mid-fifteenth century they had replaced skins and furs as warm bed coverings.

It is often said that the Vikings carried the technique to the British Isles. In her book *Rag Rugs of England and America*, Emma Tennant suggests that the Shetland Islands may have been a bridge between Scandinavia and Scotland, for they belonged to Norway until the fifteenth century and became part of Scotland only in 1469 under the marriage settlement of James III, king of Scotland, to Margaret, daughter of Kristian I of Denmark.

The rag rug tradition was strong until the early part of the twentieth century, and rugs were an essential part of a bride's dowry. These rugs were often made by 'rug women', who travelled from island to island, making rugs in return for hospitality.

In the 1930s Ann Macbeth, who had been the chief instructor in embroidery at the Glasgow School of Art between 1908 and 1920, investigated the history of rug making in Scotland, and she suggested that there were links with Viking settlers. Her evidence lay in the Scandinavian curves and scrolls that can be found carved on furniture and that were also worked as patterns, especially the borders, on rag rugs. The Viking influence is still apparent in Scotland and the north of England in design motifs, place names and dialect words.

Making woven rag rugs with ryer knots is a traditional Scandinavian technique. The loops of wool are pulled through a woven background so that they resemble the pile of an animal's fleece.

BRITAIN

Because rag rugs are utilitarian objects, originally intended to be used until they were completely threadbare and then simply discarded, hardly any early examples have survived. In addition, rug making was regarded as a working-class craft and therefore considered to be scarcely worthy of attention. It was also associated with poverty, and as people became more affluent they were often ashamed of their rugs and their associations, and so they threw them away. It has, therefore, been difficult to study the origins and development of the craft. Only very few examples, held in specialist collections, exist.

There is a tradition of making rag rugs all over the British Isles. Ann Davies, who runs the Rag Rug Society of the UK, says: 'I have met many people who can remember their parents and grandparents making rugs in ... Wales, Kent, Sussex, East Anglia,

Worcester and the East End of London.' Making hand-hooked rugs became an especially popular craft in the northeast of England. This was partly because there were many local mills and cloth factories, which meant that materials were easily available, and partly because endemic poverty led to the re-use of all old fabrics, including clothing. The heartland of British rag rug making, however, was, and to some extent still is, the area from north Lanarkshire in Scotland to Morecambe Bay, Lancashire, on the northwest coast of England.

The tools for making rugs – the hooks and frames – were usually made by men. The rug makers were usually women, although Scottish and English sailors made mats by pushing short lengths of yarn or rope through a canvas backing. These were known as 'thrummed mats', and they were used in the rigging of ships to prevent ropes from chafing.

The chequerboard pattern can be seen on hooked rugs from around the world. The colours in this example are quite dull and do, indeed, give the impression that the rug was made from worn and faded garments.

These twelve prodded designs have been turned into a mat, with the hessian background of each worked section left exposed to form a border for each pattern.

The whole family helped in rug making. The man of the house would often set up the frame, and he might draw the design on the backing fabric with a piece of charred stick taken from the fire. The children would be pressed into cutting up the old clothes that would have been saved throughout the year. When the rug was finished it would be placed in front of the fire in the best room, or parlour, while older rugs would be rotated around the house, so that the previous year's best rug would be moved to the kitchen, while the kitchen rug would be moved to the back door and so on. A well-made hooked rug is reversible, and rugs were often placed wrong side up, being turned over only on special occasions.

The Two Fishes was designed by Denis and Audrey Barker in 1974. The rug, which contains remnants of British Rail blankets, was hooked by eighty-year-old Miss F. Williams.

In Scotland rugs were usually made on a frame, which had frequently previously been used for quilting. The frames were known as stenters, from the Scottish dialect word 'stent', meaning stretch. When a frame was used, it was possible to work more quickly and easily than on hand-held rugs, and it enabled many people to work together, rather as in the tradition of the quilting bee. Most rugs were made by hooking, and they were known as 'hookies'. Friends would gather to work together, and it was not unknown for women who were not working on the rug to look after their friends' children and cook food.

The craft was widespread in poor and rural communities throughout the nineteenth century. By the 1920s and 1930s the availability of cheap, ready-made alternatives meant that it had died out in all but the most economically depressed areas, such as the northeast of England, and in isolated rural communities. During the Second World War, however, as 'make do and mend' became the watchwords, thrift led to a revival in the craft, and in the 1960s the artist Winifred Nicholson initiated a second revival of interest in Cumbrian hooked rugs by encouraging and teaching local people the techniques they need to make them again.

UNITED STATES

The first person to undertake a detailed study of rag rugs was the American architect William Winthrop Kent. His interest was initially aroused by examples that he saw in America, and he became convinced that the origins of the craft lay in Europe. This led him to correspond with Ann Macbeth. Kent's book, *The Hooked Rug*, is now out of print, but in her book *Rag Rugs* Ann Davies states that Kent concluded that hooked rugs had been known in Britain since Tudor times and that their origins were, indeed, European. Kent's research led him to the conclusion that 'it is a fact that the art was taken up more widely in, and developed more artistically in America than anywhere else', and he attributed this to the fact that the early settlers included 'both Latins and Irish [who were] instinctively and generally art-loving'.

It is believed that British settlers first took the craft to North America. There were no cotton mills, and carpets, which had to be imported, were rare and expensive. Even when the first American factory to make carpets was established in the 1820s, they were still far too expensive for most households.

When the first settlers arrived they had to use and re-use every available scrap of material. No hooked rugs were made in the United States before the 1830s, although several other techniques were used, and these are sometimes mistaken for hooking. A yarn sewn rug, for example, may look like a hooked rug from the front.

It is not known for certain when and where the first hooked rugs were made, but the technique developed in the 1840s in Quebec, Canada, and in New Hampshire and along the coast of Maine.

This early American hooked rug, which was made c.1905, was worked on a pre-stencilled pattern of the kind that first became available in the late nineteenth century. (Rug lent by Al Lamb.)

Dating from c.1905, this American hooked rug was worked on a pre-stencilled piece of hessian (burlap). Foliage motifs such as this were especially popular in the early twentieth century. (Rug lent by Al Lamb.)

It reached a peak of popularity in the 1850s, when Asian jute, which was used to make inexpensive hessian (burlap in the US, brin in Canada), was first imported into the United States. The jute was used to make sacks, and when the sacks were opened out, they could be washed and stretched on a frame as backing fabric for rugs. The size of the sacks dictated the size of the rugs.

Designs on early rugs were drawn freehand. The motifs and scenes chosen were taken from everyday life – animals, especially horses, dogs and cats, houses and wildlife, including flowers. Rugs made in coastal areas reflected life there, and designs included whales, ships, anchors, shells and ropes. Many of the patterns found in traditional quilts – the log cabin and tumbling blocks, for example – were translated into designs for rag rugs.

Hooked rugs were made in many shapes. Squares, rectangles, ovals, hexagons and octagons were all made, but one of the most popular shapes was the semicircle, which was appropriate for both the hearth and the door. Semicircular door mats often carried messages such as 'welcome' or 'call again'. Room-sized floor-coverings were rarely made, simply because they took so long to work. A smaller rug, however, could easily be made in a winter, and skilled workers could make two.

The earliest makers depended on vegetable dyes for their colours. Hemlock bark (Tsuga), peach leaves, golden rod, yellow hickory, walnut or spruce bark, onion skins, sumac, blueberry – dozens of plants were used to create a range of colours.

In 1850 hessian with pre-stencilled patterns became available for the first time. One of the first people to mass-produce and sell pre-printed hessian was Edward Sands Frost, a peddler from Biddeford, Maine. Frost's wife was an enthusiastic rag rug hooker, and after watching her at work he became interested in rug making. He drew a pattern on some sacking and showed it to a neighbour. He was soon inundated with orders for more. Frost went on to make stencils from scrap tin so that he could stamp the patterns on hessian, and he sold his handiwork from door to door.

> News of my invention of stamped rugs spread like magic. ... I at once became Frost the rug man. ... I failed to find a man who dared invest a dollar in them: in fact, people did not know what they were for, and I had to go from house to house ... for I found ladies who knew what the patterns were for.

In 1870 Frost began to print patterns in colour, and before ill-health forced him to sell his business in 1876 he had made 750 zinc stencils capable of printing 180 designs. After his death, Frost's stencils continued to be sold by mail order until 1900. They now belong to the Henry Ford Museum at Greenfield Village, Dearborn, Michigan.

By the end of the nineteenth century, with the growth of industrialization and the increasing availability of inexpensive, ready-made floor-coverings of various types, the rag rug tradition had begun to die out. At the same time, however, the influence of the Arts & Crafts Movement was beginning to be felt in England, as designers such as William Morris strove to counter the loss of craft skills arising from industrialization and the poor quality of mass-produced

Rugs depicting houses or relatives or favourite animals were often worked as reminders of childhood scenes. This Canadian rug is a family keepsake. It was worked by the hooking method and dates from the late nineteenth century.

It is not known why this hooked rug is called *Je Suis Kiki* – presumably Kiki was the name of either the cockerel or the cockerel's owner. The motif is based on a very old Canadian design, although the rug itself was worked between 1920 and 1940.

goods. The American Arts & Crafts Movement was born out of a similar dissatisfaction, and rag rug making continued, although in a more limited way, as part of the desire to sustain traditional crafts.

Shaker Rugs

The Shakers, a sect founded in England in 1747 and taken to the United States about 1774 by Anne Lee, is known for the robust simplicity of its furniture and other artefacts. Their work has come to epitomize the manufacture of high-quality products, designed so that the form perfectly serves the function of each piece. Living in isolated communities, the Shakers raised flax for textiles and sheep for wool and flannel.

As with every aspect of their lives, including the respect for property and details and care of interior furnishings, the design and manufacture of Shaker rugs and carpets were governed by the Millennial Laws of 1821, which were revised in 1845.

When brethren and sisters go up and down stairs, they should not slip their feet on the carpet or floor, but lift them up and set them down plumb, so as not to wear out the carpets or floor unnecessarily. Also when they turn at the foot of the stairs, they should not turn their feet on the floor, lest they wear holes in it.

The Millennial Laws also stated that 'the carpets in one room should be as alike as can consistently be provided, and these the deaconesses should provide'. Specific mention is made of the patterns that could be used for floor-coverings.

Carpets are admissible, but they ought to be used with discretion and made plain. Mother Lucy says two colours are sufficient for one carpet. Make one strip of red and one of grey, another of butternut and grey.

It is thought that these rugs were probably the plain woven carpets made using a rag or rag and wool combination in the weft.

They made most of the popular shapes, but with some characteristic features that identify their rugs as Shaker. The hooked rugs, for example, have rows of braiding bordering the central hooked section, and the backs may be finished with narrow Shaker-woven tape. They also made ravel-knit rugs, which are characterized by a long, shaggy pile, with the texture of unravelled knitted goods.

Hard-wearing, practical floor-coverings, such as braided, rag and fluff rugs, were made by Shaker communities and sold in their stores. Plush rugs were advertised in a catalogue of Shaker goods dating from 1870. They sold at 70 cents a square foot and were available in blue, white, yellow, gold and maroon and in any size. Also supplied were pillows and footstools to match.

Below: The two red-eyed rabbits and hearts have been worked with the date, 1884, between border-angled strips on this hooked rug, which was made by Maria Beck Warning of Ontario, Canada. The materials used include woollen knits, cotton and wool plain weave, homespun and dyed wool, stockings and sweater. The rug measures 65 x 134cm (26 x 53in).

CANADA

The French explorer Jacques Cartier sailed along the coast of Labrador in 1534, but while he thought that the harbours were excellent, he reported that the land was barren and fit only for wild beasts. By the mid-nineteenth century the coast was settled with immigrants from the British Isles, but it remained a remote, poverty-stricken place. So bad were conditions that when Dr Wilfred Grenfell was sent there in 1892 by the Charitable Mission to Deep Sea Sailors, he was appalled by what he found and spent the next year raising money to establish a mission 'for the physical and spiritual welfare of the people of Labrador and Newfoundland and for the fishermen who work on these dangerous coasts'.

In his autobiography Grenfell recorded that: 'there existed on the coast the native industry of rug hooking, to which the women were accustomed since early childhood.' At this time tuberculosis was rife, and one of Grenfell's tasks was to teach elementary hygiene. Spitting on the floor was a common occurrence, and so Grenfell paid a small sum to all those who hooked the words 'don't spit' into their rugs.

This coarsely hooked rug was made in 1911 in Ontario, Canada. The two eight-pointed stars in the central area with a heart in each corner are typical elements of Mennonite design.

To help the local economy, he set up the Village Industry Department. In 1907 Jessie Luther, a volunteer teacher of arts and crafts who was trained as an occupational therapist, joined the mission. She found the work of the local women technically excellent, but both the designs and colours of the rugs were very unattractive because of the old sacking and rags that were used to make the rugs. The rags were replaced by better quality materials, and the designs were modified to suit market tastes. By the 1930s there was a thriving export business. When Dr Grenfell went on his money-raising lecture tours, he begged his audiences to donate old silk, artificial silk and underwear. 'When your stocking runs, let it run to Labrador' became a popular slogan.

Rhoda Dawson, an artist whose designs brought a modern, abstract quality to the traditional rag rug motifs, joined the mission from England in 1930. She noted: 'The silk was dyed in vats. In one year we had nine tons.'

The rug making tradition was equally well established south of Labrador, in Newfoundland and Nova Scotia, and it survived in those regions until the early twentieth century.

Top: This detail of a coarsely hooked bedside rug shows how springy the loops on a hooked rug become when woollen fabrics are used. The complete rug measures 64 x 91cm (25 x 36in).

Bottom left: This rug is called *Memory*, and it was worked by Winifred A. Park using the hooking method. Mrs Park was the aunt of the Canadian teacher of rug hooking, Wendy Bateman.

Bottom right: This is a detail of *Tulips*, a twice woven rag rug, hooked by Wendy Bateman. For this kind of rug, which measures about 91 x 152cm (3 x 5ft), Wendy Bateman uses approximately 2.3kg (5lb) of rags.

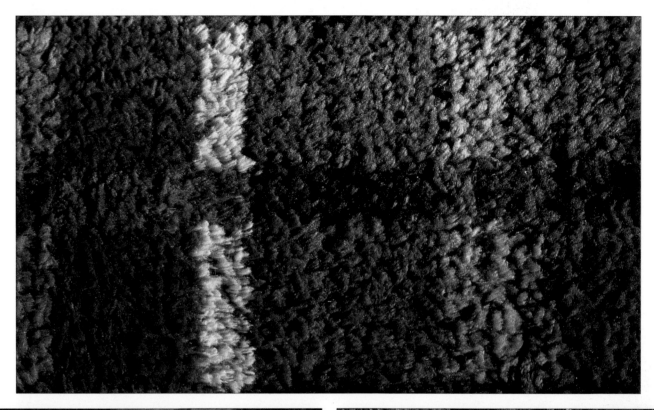

TOOLS AND MATERIALS

The basic tools and equipment that you need to begin creating your own rag rugs are few and inexpensive.

You will probably already have a sewing machine, dressmaking pins, thimbles, a tape measure, needles and thread, and a transfer pencil as well as a compass (for drawing circles) and an iron. You will, however, also need some special equipment – a frame, a hook, scissors, hessian (burlap) and, of course, rags.

FRAMES

Although it is possible to make a prodded rug without a frame, you will get better results if you hold the hessian backing material taut in a frame. Using a frame also leaves both your hands free to work. Remember that the frame must be larger than the dimensions of the rug to allow for hems and turn-ins.

In the United States, where rug hooking is a way of life for many people, there is a far wider range of frames than in Europe, where many of the frames are, in any case, relatively expensive because they tend to be hand-crafted.

Artist's Canvas Stretchers

The most inexpensive and most widely available type of frame is known as an artist's canvas stretcher – four long pieces of wood that slot together to form a rectangle.

When you are setting up a frame, it is essential that you can reach the centre of the frame while you are hooking. Therefore, while you can make the rug as wide as you wish, the depth is limited to the length of your arms. If you want to make a larger rug, you can move the rug on the stretchers or you can make several small pieces and stitch them together later.

Quilting Hoop

Many rag rug makers use a quilting hoop, which resembles a large embroidery hoop. Many of these hoops have attached legs, which means that both your hands are left free, but even if your hoop does not have legs, it is easy to support the hoop against a chair or table as you work. Make sure that the outer loop of the frame can be expanded so that it will accommodate the thickness of the completed rug.

Hooking Frame

A hooking frame consists of four long pieces of wood, two of which have a series of holes punched in the ends. The other two members, which are made of heavier wood, have holes in the ends, through which dowels or pegs can be fitted to hold the vertical members in place. These frames have the great advantage that the position of the hessian can be adjusted as you complete a section, so it is relatively easy to make longer rugs than on, say, artist's stretchers. Some hooking frames have strips of webbing attached to the long members to which the backing fabric can be stitched with strong linen thread.

HOOKS AND PRODDERS

After a frame, the main tool you will need is a rug hook. This is very similar to a metal crochet hook but has a sharper point and a handle. The handles vary in shape – they can be long and thin or short and round – and the hook sizes range from no. 1, which is for the finest strips, to no. 10, which is for the widest strips.

A prodder is similar to a hook but, unlike a hook, does not have a barb on the end. The point on the end is used to push or 'prod' rags through the hessian foundation fabric.

A shuttle hook or speed shuttle is used to make a series of loops through the foundation fabric. These hooks are quicker to use than a traditional hook, but they are not as easy to find as ordinary hooks or prodders. However, they are available through some specialist suppliers, so you may feel it worthwhile searching round for one.

Right: Lizzie Reakes making a rag rug using the hooked method and working on a frame.

Prodders come in a variety of sizes and shapes. They range from simple sticks with a tapered end to specially made brass or steel prodders with shaped wooden handles. It is even possible to use a large nail.

Different types and sizes of rug hooks are available.
They resemble crochet hooks but often have a wooden handle.
A rug hook also usually has a sharper barb than a crochet hook to
catch hold of the rag strips from beneath the work more securely.

If you prefer your rugs to have a more woven look, you might want to consider using a locker-needle hook. This implement has a large-eyed darning needle at one end and a crochet hook at the other. The hooked end is used to make a series of loops, and fabric is pulled through the loops with the needle, which 'locks' the loops in place and prevents them from falling back through the foundation fabric.

Materials and Fabrics

The earliest rag rugs were made of clothes that were so worn they could no longer be passed on or repaired. They were made from old aprons, dresses, shirts and trousers, which meant that they were largely cotton. The years of wear gave them their own distinctive, mellow colours. However, a problem with cotton rag rugs is that they tend to flatten because there is no natural spring in cotton.

The preferred material for rag rugs is woollen fabric, which is durable and has texture. New wool is comparatively expensive, but old woollen garments and blankets, picked up from car-boot sales and jumble sales, and cast-offs from family and friends will be perfect for your purposes. Wool also accepts dyes easily and well.

When you are cutting wool into strips, the only rule to remember is that the tighter the weave of the fabric, the thinner it should be cut. Looser weaves should, ideally, be pre-shrunk and matted or felted before being cut into strips.

Patterned wools, such as herringbone, tweeds, tartans and so on, create interesting designs, so do not rule them out.

If you are making a rug, make sure that the materials you use are hard-wearing and durable, which probably means sticking to traditional wools and cottons, although do not exclude velour, organdie, satin, synthetics, terry towelling or even Lurex. If you are planning to make a wall-hanging or cushion, however, you could try almost anything – including foil, crisp packets and leather. Keep bits and pieces that are of sentimental value and insert them into a work.

Designs for hooked rugs can be more detailed than those worked by prodding. It is, however, easy to get a striped effect when you use lines of plain fabrics, so avoid this by using patterned fabrics such as checks, plaids and dog-toothed tweeds. Prodded rugs, on the other hand, can look almost Impressionistic.

Experiment with colours and textures as you work. If you are unsure, about something, it is easy to remove the offending colour and replace it with something else. If you want to use less sturdy fabrics, such as velvet, support them with a stronger one such as wool.

Margaret Docherty's studio in the heart of Gloucestershire is a rag rug worker's paradise, overflowing with rags of velvet, corduroy, cottons and wools of every imaginable shade. The pattern of the *Turkish Diamond* cushion cover was inspired by her travels in the Far East.

FOUNDATION MATERIALS

A foundation material is needed so that the rag strips are attached to something. This material must be both durable and have a loose weave.

The base material used to hook on is hessian (burlap). This is inexpensive and is available on rolls, so you can buy fairly large pieces. The ideal weight is sold as 12oz hessian, but if you are a beginner, try 10oz hessian, which has a slightly looser weave. Before you buy, look carefully at the hessian to make sure that there are no breaks in the fibres, which could lead to holes in your finished work.

An alternative is cotton monk's cloth, which is widely available in North America. This has a tighter weave than hessian but is a tougher fabric, and it will last longer. Other possible foundation materials are linen, which is rather expensive, or heavy, loose-weave cotton. You might even consider an open-weave synthetic fabric.

You can use any fabric you wish provided that it is hard wearing, will not stretch and has a weave that is loose enough to hook or prod through.

When you are working on your rug, you have to secure the foundation fabric to the frame. A staple gun is a convenient way of holding the fabric in place. Make sure that the fabric is absolutely straight as it is stretched over the frame by inserting the staples very close together, especially at the corners. If you do not have a staple gun, use drawing pins.

If you use a shuttle hook, it is doubly important that the foundation fabric is securely attached to your frame, and you can use webbing, which is stitched to the hessian, and a strong thread to lace the backing to the frame.

A shuttle hook is being used to work these lines of colour. There is no need to work in lines across the background fabric.
Use the outline of the motifs as a guide for the first row of loops, then work the next row close to the first.

Left: This Rigby strip cutter comes from Maine, USA. Rug hooking is a popular and widely practised pastime in North America, and many rug making accessories are more widely available there than in Europe. This particular model of strip cutter can be set to produce a range of widths, although about 1cm (³/8 in) wide is suitable for most hooking.

RUG BINDING EQUIPMENT

You will need wide cotton binding to bind the edges of your finished rug. The binding should match the main colour of the rug as closely as possible, and if you cannot obtain the correct shade, you might want to consider dyeing the binding. Commercial binding will shrink when it is washed, so buy more than you actually need.

You will also need a carpet needle and strong thread with which to stitch the binding to the rug. An alternative to a needle and thread is a strong, rubber-based fabric glue such as Copydex.

You may also wish to seal the back of the finished rug to prevent threads from working loose. You can apply a coat of latex or PVA adhesive to the back, although some makers feel that it is best not to seal the rug because the sealant tends to cause the rug to rot in the long term. However, other makers like to seal the backs of their rugs to secure the loops and give a harder wearing finish.

CUTTING EQUIPMENT

You will need a pair of sharp dressmaking scissors with long blades to cut the foundation fabric, strips of fabric and any trimming materials.

You will also find a pair of napping scissors useful for trimming off loops and for fine detailing. They are also good for shearing loops to give a velvety effect to the pile.

A strip cutting machine will allow you to cut strips quickly and accurately. These are more widely available in North America than in Europe, but they are becoming easier to find. The machines can usually be clamped to a work surface, and the cutting mechanism is operated by turning a hand crank. The variety of interchangeable cutter wheels enables you to cut several layers of strips at the same time, and the distance between them can be adjusted so that strips of different widths can be cut.

DRAWING TOOLS

To draw or transfer a design to the foundation material you will need some drawing equipment.

Tracing paper or greaseproof paper and carbon paper can be used to trace a design on to the backing fabric. Alternatively, use graph paper to scale up your design before you transfer it to the material.

Use a soft pencil to trace the design, and go over the outlines with a heavy felt-tipped marker pen because the pencil lines will not be clear enough for you to work with.

If you need to make a template to transfer a design, cut it out from stiff card and hold it in place with masking tape.

TECHNIQUES

✳

Of the various types of rag rug, those made by hooking or prodding are the most popular. There are so many regional names for both these techniques, including hooky, proddy, proggy, bodged and clipped, that an outsider may think that the craft is more complicated than it really is. When you are working with any kind of rag rug, remember that alterations can be made at any time during the making process. It is easy to remove a colour if it looks wrong – simply pull the rag strips or pieces out of the backing fabric.

HOOKED RUGS

A hooked rug is worked from the top, with the backing fabric stretched on a frame. A long strip of fabric is held under the foundation material, and a hook, rather like a long crochet hook, is pushed through the front of the foundation material to catch the strip of fabric held at the back. The strip is pulled through to the front to create a loop. The process is repeated until the front is covered with a pattern of loops. The end of the fabric strip is always pulled through to the front to prevent the loops from unravelling. When the design is complete, the loops are sometimes cut close to the backing fabric to create a pile. This technique was most often used in the United States and Canada.

There is no right or wrong way to hook – different people use different methods. However, you should become familiar with a basic technique before you begin, then, as you gain experience and become confident, you can hook in your own way.

There is no special order in which you should work, although it is probably easier to hook through the outlines and then to fill them with colour rather than working across the foundation fabric and having continually to change colours. If you are not certain that you have sufficient of one particular colour, it is probably best to begin in the centre and to work outwards in both directions.

If you are right-handed, hold the hook in your right hand as you would hold a pencil. Hold the rag strip between the thumb and forefinger of your left hand under the foundation fabric in the approximate place where the hook will enter.

Insert the hook at the starting point by pushing it firmly through the hessian. The hole made should be large enough for the hook to be pulled back through. Catch the end of the rag strip and pull it up through to the front with the hook so that there is an end about 2.5cm (1in) long. Push the hook through to the back of the hessian two threads along, catch the strip in the hook and pull through the first loop. Remove the hook from the loop and then push the hook back through a further two threads along. Pull through the next loop. Continue working in this way until about 2.5cm (1in) of rag strip is left. Pull this up to the top. You will find it quicker if you do not try to feed the strip to the hook; instead, allow the hook to find the strip.

Begin hooking with the next rag strip. Hold it under the base fabric and pull the tail through the same hole as the end of the previous strip. Then continue hooking as before.

The reverse side of your work will look as if it is covered in rows of running stitches. If there are loops on the back, it means that you are not pulling the rag strip up to the front properly. The loops you make

When you begin hooking, hold a strip of fabric in one hand under
the backing fabric. With the hook in the other hand and working
from the front of the hessian, push the hook through the back.

Catch the fabric strip in the hook and pull an end, about 2.5cm
(1in) long, through to the front. Move the hook along by
four or five threads.

Push the hook through to the back of the hessian
and pull through a loop from the strip beneath. Pull the
loop to the height you require. The height should be the
same as the previously formed loops.

Move the hook along by four or five threads and push it
through to the back of the hessian. Pull through another loop.
Continue working in this way, pulling the end of the
strip through to the front.

When you have finished hooking a rug, you can give it a chenille-type finish by shearing it. Hold your scissors parallel to the backing fabric and snip across the loops.

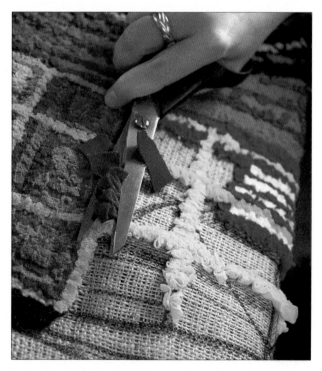

If you want a textured surface, use your scissors to shear wavy lines across your work rather than trimming straight across.

should be approximately as high as they are wide so that they create a firm pile. You can vary the heights of the loops to create different textural effects.

Leave about two threads between each row of hooking. If the loops are too tightly packed together they will strain the backing and the rug will not wear well.

If your strips are quite wide the edges of a loop may come through crookedly. If this happens, pull the loop right up, straighten it and pull it back from underneath until it is level with the other loops.

When you work, make sure that you do not carry strips from one section of the backing to another. If your hook catches on one of these strips as you work, you may accidentally pull up a whole row of hooking.

If you are hooking a solid circle of colour, fill in the area by working in a spiral from the centre outwards. Follow the contours of outlines as you fill in patterns to create textural effect. The way in which shapes are worked can affect they way they look. For example, a corner can be more or less defined depending on whether a particular point is pushed in or pulled out.

Trim off the tails at the front from time to time so that the ends are level with the loops.

PRODDED RUGS

A prodded or poked rug is worked from the back. Although these rugs can be worked without a frame, you will find it easier to work if the hessian is taut in a frame. The technique involves making holes with a pointed tool, a prodder, made of wood or metal, and pushing small rectangles of clippings of fabric through the backing material to create a thick, shaggy pile at the front. The designs that can be worked with this technique are largely limited to stripes or marble effects, and you can achieve an almost pointillist effect. There are some notable exceptions, however, as can be seen in the work of Ben Hall (see pages 86–87).

Prodded rugs are worked from the back. Begin by using a prodder to make a hole in hessian at the point you want to start.

Push the end of a short strip of rag through the hole so that about half comes through to the front.

Move the prodder along by four or five threads (it may have to be more if the rag pieces are from a thick fabric) and push the prodder through the hessian from the back to the front to make a second hole.

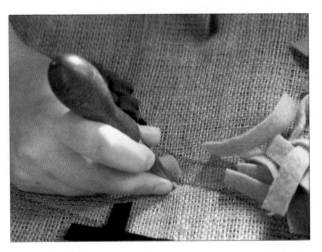

Push the rest of the rag strip through to the other side, and use the hand that is under the hessian to check that the two ends are more or less the same length. Continue working in this way to create an even pile on the front and rows of neat, flat loops on the back.

The strips of rag used are shorter than those needed for a hooked rug. When each piece is folded in two, it is the depth of the pile, although the pieces can be trimmed when a rug is complete.

The side of the hessian foundation fabric on which the design is drawn is the back of the finished rug, which means that the pattern will be the reverse of what you have drawn. It is important to remember to take this into account when you transfer your design to the hessian.

Because hessian tends to have an uneven weave, pull a thread to get a straight edge. If you wish, before you begin turn under a hem all round of about 1.5cm (1/2 in) and machine stitch it in place, stitching through the double thickness of cloth. You can prod rag pieces through this thickness so there will be no finishing to do at the end.

Working from your design and using a grid if you are making a large rug, rough out the outlines in chalk on the wrong side of the hessian. When you are satisfied with the outline, go over the lines with a felt-tipped pen or a chinagraph pencil. If you are making a light coloured rug, it is important not to use too dark a pen. If your motifs are large, it is sometimes easier to use a template.

Use strong thread to stitch the hessian to the webbing of the frame or pin or staple it in place. Make sure that it is perfectly straight and square on the frame so that there is no distortion. When you are working with a hooking frame, only about 45cm (18in) of the hessian needs to be exposed. The remainder of the hessian can be wound around the frame and then, as each section is completed, it can be wound on to expose the next area.

With the back of the hessian towards you, take the prodder in your right hand (if you are right-handed) and hold it as you would hold a pencil. Push it through the starting point of the hessian to make a hole. Remove the prodder and place a rag strip over the hole you have just made. Use the prodder to push one end of the rag through from the back to the front. With your other hand under the hessian, pull the strip half-way through to what will be the right side of your work.

Two threads from the starting point, use the prodder to make a second hole, then push through the other end of the rag strip. With your other hand, pull through the rag so that the two ends are level.

Use the prodder to insert the end of a second piece of rag into the second hole that you have made, pulling it through to the other side, and continuing as before. Cover the rug in this way. Two rag strips will come through every hole you make, and this creates a firm material and helps prevent pieces of rag from falling out. If you are using thick material you may have to make a new hole, close to the first one, to push the second clipping through.

When you have finished, remove the rug from the frame, turn it over and trim the whole surface, taking off as little as possible from the ends of the rags to give a neat pile.

Ali Rhind in her studio. The piece she is working on is stretched on a frame and is being made using the hooked method of working.

ALI RHIND'S METHOD

Every rug maker has his or her own preferred methods of working. Ali Rhind (see pages 97–100) uses a method of prodding that is very speedy because one hand stays below the hessian all the time.

Ali prepares the frame as above and cuts 7.5cm (3in) strips of fabric into pieces. She likes to work with 10oz hessian in her frame, which is supported on two trestles, but you could rest it on chairs or tables. She keeps her left hand under the frame. With the prodder and middle finger of her right hand she lifts up a piece of fabric and pokes it half-way through with the prodder. With her left hand she catches the fabric piece and pulls it down to the correct height.

The next hole is made five threads away, which is the equivalent of just less than 1cm (about 3/8in), and the other end of the fabric is presented to the hole and pushed through. The other end of the fabric catches the second end and checks that the two ends are level.

The second clipping is pushed into the same hole as the second end of the first clipping, and the process is repeated until the hessian is covered.

Detail of a modern chair pad made using the hooked method, then trimmed closely with scissors to create a cropped pile.
This technique is a modern equivalent to shirring.

SHIRRED RUGS

Shirred rugs, which are sometimes known as chenille rugs (from the French word for caterpillar), were made between about 1820 and 1850. There are three main techniques.

The first method involves taking a line of running stitches down the centre of a strip of cloth. The thread is then pulled up to gather the strip, which gives a shirred or caterpillar-like effect. The gathered strip is stitched to the backing fabric. Other caterpillars are added until the backing fabric is covered.

The second method uses bias-cut strips of fabric. These are folded in half, and the folded edge is stitched to the backing fabric. The strips are stitched as close together as possible so that the raw edges form a pile.

The third type of shirred rug is made by taking a row of stitches across the centre of wide strips of fabric. The fabric is drawn into loops then stitched again, with each loop being as close as possible to the ones next to it. Again, the completed rag rug will have a close, regular pile.

BRAIDED RUGS

This type of rug was first made in the United States between about 1830 and 1850. They are, as the name suggests, made from strips of fabric that are braided or plaited together. The braids are then stitched together to form a rectangle or coiled and stitched together to form an oval or circle. No backing fabric is required.

Probably the only specific tool you need to make a simple braided rug is a large safety pin – a kilt pin or nappy pin would be ideal.

You will need long strips of fabric, ideally about 2m (6ft) long and 7.5cm (3in) wide. So that the strips do not get tangled as you work, roll up the strips, leaving an end to work with, and secure each roll with a dressmaking pin. You can unroll the strips a little at a time as you work.

Use the safety pin to fasten together the three loose ends of your strips of fabric. So that the braid does not move around as you work, hook the pin over a wall hook or drawer knob. Before you begin to work, roll the raw edges of each strip inside and

Braiding is a simple yet effective way of making rag rugs. No special equipment is needed – the strips are simply plaited and the braids are stitched together in a spiral. Because there are no loose ends, braided rugs are the only kind of rag rug that can be washed in a machine.

This detail illustrates the way in which chain stitch, worked in metallic embroidery thread and following the contours of the rug, has been used to embellish a braided rug.

away from what will be the front of the rug. Bring the right-hand strip over the centre strip, then the left-hand strip over the strip in the centre, and continue to braid. Do not pull the strips too tightly – you are aiming for a smooth, even plait. Make sure that you turn in the raw edges as you work, unrolling the strips a little at a time as needed. When you reach the end hold the ends of the braid together with a pin.

Some people prefer to press and sew in the raw edges of the strips before they begin to braid, and although this is time consuming it does give an extra-neat finish. It is not essential, however.

Continue to braid lengths of rag in this way until you have sufficient for a rug. Place the braids side by side on a flat surface to form a rectangle and, with a large needle and strong thread, stitch one side of one braid to the side of the next one. Repeat the process until you have sewn all the strips together.

The next step is to neaten the raw edges. Take a

piece of fabric and place it, right side down and raw edges together, over one short end of the braids. Run a row of even basting stitches along the edge. Turn the fabric over to the wrong side, turn in the raw edge and secure it with a row of stitches. Repeat at the other end.

To make a border for the rug, braid a length of rags sufficiently long to go around the entire edge of the rug. Taper one end of the braid neatly, then sew it around the edge of the rug to finish it off.

An alternative method is to coil the braids into a spiral, stitching the outside edge of the braid to the inside edge of the next braid as you work. If you choose to do this, you will need to stitch lengths of braid together end to end to create one very long strip that you can wind into a rug, rather than stitching them side to side.

SHUTTLE HOOKED RUGS

The technique of shuttle hooking gives the same results as traditional hand hooking, but the method differs. A shuttle hook works rather like a gun, 'shooting' the rag strips into loops, which is, of course, much quicker than hand hooking.

If you are going to use a shuttle hook, you will have to transfer the design to the hessian and attach the hessian backing to a frame in rather different ways from those needed for hand hooking.

As with the prodding method, you work from the wrong side of the foundation material, which means that you should reverse the design. It is particularly important to remember that the design will be reversed if you are planning to include words in it. Trace the outlines of your chosen motifs or patterns on to tracing paper or greaseproof paper and then go over the outlines on the reverse of the paper with a soft pencil. Place the paper, wrong side down, on the hessian, and go over the outlines so that the pencil lines are transferred to the hessian. You will probably then need to go over the outlines with a felt-tipped marker pen.

Stretch the foundation material securely on a frame. Because the rug is worked from the back, the design has to be transferred to the reverse of the hessian. Thread a strip of fabric through the eye of the hook and through the loop on the side.

If you are right-handed, hold one side of the shuttle hook in your left hand and the side with the eye in your right hand, then push the eye through the hessian at the point you want to begin working.

Keeping your left hand still, push the other side of the shuttle hook through to the front of the hessian and then slide it back, aligning the two sides of the shuttle.

Move the shuttle hook a little way along the line of your outline and repeat the previous two steps to make a second loop. Continue working in this way, replacing the rag strip as necessary.

Next, attach the hessian backing to the frame. Use a carpet needle and strong thread to stitch a length of wide binding or webbing to the two short sides of the hessian. Staple these two bound edges to the frame, stretching the hessian as taut as possible across the frame, but at the same time making sure that the threads are perfectly straight. Use strong thread to lace the two long sides to the horizontal members of the frame. It is important that the hessian is firmly held.

Prop the frame against a wall, with the back facing outwards, so that the shuttle hook can pierce the foundation with no danger to yourself.

Thread the shuttle hook with a rag strip, taking the strip through the eye and the two support rings. Hold the shuttle hook with both hands, leaving the end of the rag strip free. Slide the needle of the shuttle hook into the hessian backing fabric at your starting point, then slide the top half of the shuttle into the hessian. This action creates a loop on the front of the hessian, but from the back it will look like a running stitch. Continue to follow the outline of the design, filling in the different areas as you would if you were hand hooking.

CHAIN STITCH WITH RAGS

Although this is not a conventional technique, using rag strips to create rows of chain stitch is an unusual and effective way of decorating a hooked rug. The technique is used in the Hausa-shaped Chain Stitch Hanging by Margaret Docherty, which is included as a project on pages 119–120, and Jenni Stuart-Anderson has used it in her eagle rugs. The effect is similar to that of embroidered chain stitch.

Use strips of rags and a hook – you may find that a crochet hook is sufficient if you are using fine strips. Insert the hook in the hessian and bring the end of a strip to the front. Insert the hook two strands in front of the first hole, pull through a loop

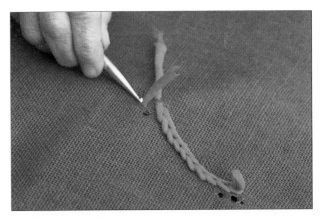

Although chain stitching is not a conventional rag rug technique, it looks very effective. Work from the front, with the hessian stretched on a frame, and use a rag hook or an ordinary crochet needle. Bring the end of a strip of fabric through to the front.

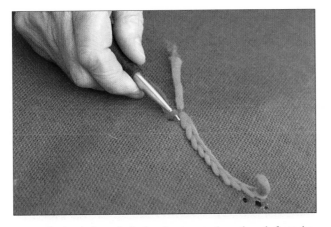

Insert the hook through the hessian two or three threads from the first hole and bring a loop of the fabric strip through to the front.

Still with the loop on the hook, insert the hook two or three threads from the second hole. Bring a second loop through.

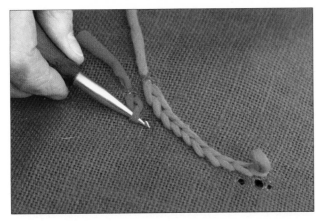

Slip the first loop over the second, forming the first 'link' in the chain. This lies on the surface of the hessian, just like an embroidered chain stitch.

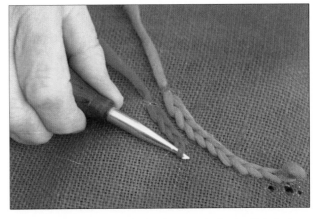

With the second loop on the hook, insert the hook a little further along the line of your pattern and pull a third loop through. Slip off the second loop. Continue in this way to create neat chains.

and, still with the loop on the hook, insert the hook two strands further on. Bring a second loop through to the front and slip the first loop over it. Continue with the process, working in straight lines, curves and spirals.

WOVEN RAG RUGS

The early settlers in North America took with them from Europe the small tools required for making rag rugs, but it seems that only very few looms were taken, probably because of the impracticality of transporting such large items. As soon as families were established, however, it is likely that looms were constructed in the same styles that had been so familiar in Europe, and it seems that they were often shared not only within individual households, but also in local communities, and a loom would be taken from house to house as different families wanted to use it.

Although today they are less often used in the making of rag rugs, looms can be still be used to weave rugs. One contemporary rag rug artist, Alison Morton, uses a loom (see page 93). Because it is more difficult to create patterns in woven rugs than in hooked rugs, Alison makes patterns by tying together different strips of fabric on the warp as she weaves. This causes the colours to fuse together, giving an almost Impressionist effect.

A small rag rug can be woven on a picture frame, and you could make several small pieces and join them together. Artist's canvas stretchers are ideal for larger projects, or, if you prefer, you can easily make a frame to exactly match your own requirements from pieces of timber.

Alison Morton used both the plain weave and twill methods to make these woven rugs. Plain weave can be worked on a two-shaft loom, but a twill weave needs to be worked on a loom with at least four shafts. One shaft is raised at a time so that the weft, which is created from rag strips, is placed under a different group of warp threads each time a row is worked.

The fabrics you use for weaving must be washed and ironed before they are cut into strips. To avoid having too many frayed edges and to give the fabric a certain degree of elasticity, make bias strips by cutting diagonally from selvage to selvage. Using bias-cut strips has the additional advantage that their natural 'pull' causes the raw edges to turn inwards as you work, giving a neater effect.

The width of the strips will depend on the kind of finish you want. The thinner the strips, the more delicate the finished piece will look. When you begin to weave, you do not need to join the strips together – just overlap them as you work.

In addition to the frame and strips of fabric, you will find it helpful (but not essential) to have the following items.

• Shed stick: the gap through which the weft passes is called a shed, and you can speed up the process by threading a shed stick under alternate warp threads. When it is turned on its side, it will create a larger gap, which makes it easier for you to pass the fabric through the correct warp thread. Make a shed stick from a strip of wood that is wider than the loom. Sand the edges smooth and drill a hole in each end. Tie a length of string through one hole, insert the stick in the loom, pass the string over the warp threads and tie it in the other hole. This stops the stick from slipping out but allows it to be moved up and down.

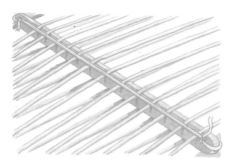

A shed stick is used to raise alternate warp threads so that the shuttle holding the weft threads can be passed easily from one side to the other.

• Shuttle: a piece of card or wood, cut in an H-shape, is a convenient way to hold the weft fabric and guide it through the warp threads. You might find it helpful to have a separate shuttle for each colour you use.

A simple shuttle can be cut from a piece of card. It is easier to pass the weft thread under and over the warp threads if it is wound on a shuttle.

Preparing the Frame

Lay your wooden frame on a flat surface and hammer large-headed nails or tacks into the two short sides. Space the nails evenly along the outside edge of the frame so that they are about 1cm (¹/₂ in) apart. Insert a second row of nails on both short sides, below the first row and positioned between the nails on the outside row.

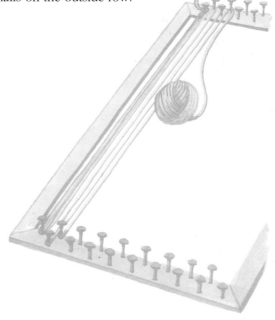

When you are stringing a frame with warp threads, make sure that you have a double thread at both sides to give a firm selvage. This will strengthen the edges of the work.

The nails are used to hold the warp threads – that is, the threads that run along the length of the rug – in position. For rag rugging an ideal warp thread is dish-cloth cotton. Tie the thread to the top left-hand nail and take it down to the bottom left-hand nail. Take it up again to the same top left-hand nail and down to the bottom left-hand nail to give a double thread, which will form a strong selvage edge. Now take the thread up to the second top nail and back down to the second nail on the bottom. Then take it up to the third top nail. Continue in this way until you reach the last nails on the right-hand side, when you should double the thread to make another strong selvage.

Preparing to Weave

Cut a piece of card that is slightly wider than the overall width of your loom and about 7.5cm (3in) deep. Weave the card through the lower end of the warp threads.

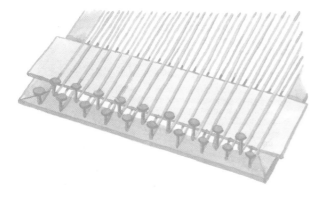

Use a piece of card to keep the first line of weft threads straight.

Cut a piece of thread that is four times as long as the width of the loom, fold it in two and pass one end under the first double (left-hand) warp thread. Weave it across and over the double warp thread at the other side. Work a second row in the same way, but working from right to left. These rows will hold the rug when it is cut from the loom.

Weaving

Beginning at the left-hand side, thread the rag strip over the selvage threads and under the next thread. Pull the rag through, leaving an end of about 10cm (4in), which will be tucked into the next row. Proceed to weave the rag strip across the warp thread, working first from left to right, then from right to left. You may find it helpful to use a wide-toothed comb to help push the weft firmly down as you work so that the warp threads are covered and so that the weaving is straight and even.

On each row, make sure that the rag strip is long enough to reach to at least the centre, where it is easier to disguise any joins. Overlap the two ends by about six warp threads so that the weft is held firmly in place. Push any ends through to the back.

Finishing Off

When you reach the end, weave two rows of doubled warp thread as at the beginning. Ideally, leave about 7.5cm (3in) of warp thread unwoven to match the depth of the card at the beginning. Cut all the warp threads from the nails and divide them into small groups before plaiting them to make a tidy fringe. Knot the ends to stop them unravelling, then stitch in any loose ends or push them through to the back of the rug.

BINDING AND FINISHING

Regardless of which technique you used to make your rag rug, you will want to finish it off neatly by binding the edges and, possibly, by adding a backing to provide extra strength.

Before you attach any binding to a rug always wash it because binding tends to shrink. You might also want to consider dyeing it to match the rug (see pages 53–59).

Use a carpet needle and strong thread to stitch on the binding. Begin half-way along one edge, with the binding on the right side of the rug, and hem stitch the binding to the hessian, working as close as

As can be seen here, the reverse of a prodded rug looks much neater when the design is worked in evenly spaced rows rather than in patterns. Strips of binding fabric or hessian can be stitched or glued around the turned-back raw edges to give a neat, strong finish.

possible to the last row of hooking. Ease the binding around the corners.

When you have attached the binding all the way around the rug, trim off the excess hessian to about 5cm (2in) from the binding. Snip off the corners at an angle. Turn the hessian back to the wrong side of the rug and carefully tack or baste it in place. Pull the binding over the edge of the hessian and hem it down all around, mitring the corners and overstitching the angles.

Another way of finishing off the rug is simply to turn under the hessian all the way around to make a neat hem on the reverse. Slip stitch it in place, taking care to mitre the corners and to overstitch the angles of the mitres.

There is some discussion about the advisability of applying latex to the back of a rug, and it is entirely a matter of personal preference. If you decide to add latex, take the rug from the frame if you have used one and trim the hessian backing to leave a border of about 5cm (2in) all round. Lay the rug, right side down, on a flat surface and turn down the edges all round, holding the hem down with a latex adhesive. Take a piece of backing material – another piece of hessian – that is slightly smaller than the rug and use the latex to stick it to the reverse of the rug. Neaten the edges by sticking carpet binding over the raw edges, mitring the corners.

If your rag rug is going to be used as a wall-hanging, back it with a fabric such as calico. Lay the finished rug face down on a flat surface and place the backing fabric over the back. Beginning in the centre of one edge, turn down a hem as you work along, pinning it in place as you go. At corners, mitre the fabric as neatly as you can. Make sure that the backing is not too taut or it will cause the rug to curl up. Use strong thread to slip stitch the backing fabric in place.

Before you turn a rug into a wall-hanging, you may want to sew loops, made from tape, along the top edge so that you can insert a rod from which the rug can be suspended.

TRANSFERRING A DESIGN

Before you place the hessian or burlap foundation on the frame (see below) you need to transfer the design to it.

If you are confident of your skills as a draughtsman, you can draw the design on the base fabric freehand. Use a very soft pencil at first, then go over it with a dark, waterproof felt-tipped marker pen.

If you see a suitable design in a book or magazine or on a poster or card, enlarge it on a photocopier. You may have to make several enlargements to achieve a suitable size, and turning the enlarged image through 90 degrees each time helps to prevent the image from distorting as it is enlarged. Then square up the design. Use a ruler and pencil to draw a grid of equal squares over the photocopied image. Using the grid as a guide, transfer the image to graph paper. (Alternatively, photocopy the image

The rug on the left was worked by the hooked method, while the one on the right shows the same design worked by the prodded method. This kind of rug frame is one of the most useful models because it can be easily adjusted to fit the size of the backing fabric. The hessian is laced firmly to the strips of webbing that are attached to the long cross-pieces. The hessian in the frame has been pre-printed with the design and is available in kit form.

directly on to graph paper.) Using this as guide, draw the image on the hessian. If you prefer, place a sheet of carbon paper, face down, between the graph paper and foundation material and trace over the image. Go over the transferred lines with a felt-tipped marker pen.

You can cut templates from stiff card and draw around these, or you could use a transfer pencil to draw the design on a piece of tracing or greaseproof paper. When you are happy with the design, pin the paper to the hessian, transfer side down, and go over it with a hot iron. This will transfer the outlines of the design to the material. If the lines are faint, go over them with a felt-tipped marker pen. Use a dark marker pen only if working with dark coloured rags.

USING A FRAME

If you are going to use a frame, you must stretch the hessian base taut to make it easier to insert the hook or prodder. When you stretch the hessian on the frame, make sure that it is perfectly straight and even. If it is not, the finished rug may look lopsided when it is taken from the frame. If you are going to use a shuttle hook, see page 34 for guidelines on attaching the hessian to a frame; for hand hooking follow the instructions below.

Staple or pin one side to one of the short sides of the frame first, placing the staples or pins close together. Then work along a long side. Then pin the hessian to the other short side, pulling it tightly and evenly. Finally, pin the remaining long side.

LOOKING AFTER YOUR RUGS

By the very nature of their construction, hooked rugs are delicate and require careful treatment.

In the first place, decide if your rug is being made for practical or decorative reasons. If you are making a rug for practical purposes, it should be as sturdy as possible. The best materials for such rugs are derived from natural fibres, especially wool, which is hard wearing. Rags from wool blankets are ideal. However, if you are more interested in making a decorative object, place it where it will not be subject to too much traffic – this rules out the hall and doorways. Walking on rag rugs flattens and wears the materials, making the fibres settle and more prone to collecting dirt. If your rug is very delicate, use it as a wall-hanging, mounting it on a board so that the weight is evenly supported.

As soon as you have completed your rug, use a protective spray. Proprietary suede and leather sprays should help the rug to repel stains and dirt. Apply several layers of spray, allowing each one to dry before applying the next, and then check that it has been sealed with a drop of water. If the rug absorbs the water, you have not sealed it properly, so more sprays are needed.

For light cleans, to remove dust and surface dirt, use a brush and sweep both the front and back of the rug. Do not shake or beat the rug because the threads of the hessian base will break.

Old rugs need special care, even if they are only being moved from one place to another, because the hessian threads are so much weaker than the woollen rags that they often simply disintegrate.

Many people would be horrified at the thought of using a vacuum cleaner on a rag rug, but as long as you are very careful it can be done. Never, however, use a brush-action vacuum cleaner because it will not only weaken the hessian but also pull out sections of hooking.

There are two possible ways of cleaning a hooked rug with a vacuum cleaner. The first is to place a

This rag rug was worked by Ben Hall by the prodding method. He used rags from faded stone-washed and indigo denim garments, and managed to make the central motif appear to be almost three-dimensional. Appropriately, the rug is called *Carpet Beater*.

Prodded rugs tend to be heavier and bulkier than hooked rugs of the same size. Because they are held together only by the foundation fabric, they should never be put in a washing machine. When you need to clean a rag rug, hang it up and beat it.

piece of sheeting between the cleaner and rug so that the dirt particles are drawn through the mesh of the sheeting but the fragile fibres are not drawn through. The second is to use the upholstery attachment on a medium setting so that the air suction removes dirt with the least possible agitation.

If there is a small stain, try to remove it straight-away by soaking it up with kitchen paper or a towel. Sponge the area with cold water, but take care that you do not get the rug too wet and that you do not scrub too hard. If the stain is stubborn, use a solution of white vinegar and water or of household ammonia and water, wipe it on to the stain and blot up the excess moisture. Some rag rug makers recommend that a toothbrush be used to clean the surface of a rug using a gentle scrubbing action.

If you want to wash a rag rug, fill a bath with cool water and some liquid detergent and lay the rug in the bath, keeping it as flat as possible. 'Knead' the rug gently so that the water penetrates the fibres, but take care that you do not scrub or twist the rug because this will break the threads in the hessian base. Allow the rug to soak for a short time, then knead it again. Empty out the bath, leaving the rug in place, then refill it with clean, cool water and a little more detergent. Soak and knead, and repeat the process until the water remains clean. Allow the rug to drain over the bath, then place it on a flat surface and leave it to dry, which could take several days. Do not wring and squeeze it.

Under no circumstances should you try to wash a hooked rag rug in a washing machine. Even the lowest setting is too strong for a rug – it will just fall to pieces. Braided or plaited rugs can be washed in a machine, however.

Before you store a hooked rug, make sure it is clean and completely dry. Place the rug face down on the floor, lay a sheet of bubble wrap over it, then roll it up with the right side facing out. Always roll rugs with the top facing outwards because this places

the least possible strain on the hessian base and makes it less likely to weaken and split.

When you have rolled up the rug in bubble wrap, wrap it in a white sheet with one or two moth balls or insecticidal flakes, and store it in a dark, dry place where the temperature is constant. Avoid places that are subject to extreme changes of temperature and avoid humid places, which will give rise to mildew.

If a prodded rug is closely packed and has been completely backed, it can be hand washed in a bath of warm water with a few drops of detergent. Knead it gently until the water runs clear and allow it to dry in the bath for a while before hanging it on an airer to finish drying.

COLOUR AND DYEING

Colour surrounds us. Everywhere we look we
see colour, and everything we touch has colour.
It stimulates our senses, and it affects our moods and
attitudes without our being aware that it is doing so.
Finding colours and a colour scheme for your rag
rugs is perhaps one of the most important aspects of
preparation, and it is important that you are as happy
with the colours you choose when you have finished
your work as you were when you started. Colours
are known to have specific psychological effects –
blue is tranquil, yellow is invigorating, green is
soothing and red is stimulating, for example.

No colour can ever be seen in isolation,
however. When one colour is placed beside another,
we perceive both in a different way. Even the
circumstances in which a colour is seen can affect
our perception of it, as all colours are part of our
experience, and we react, albeit subconsciously, to
this. Descriptions of the same shade by a group of
people can vary widely from person to person, and
it is known that individual colours have different
associations in various countries and cultures.

We are surrounded by nature's palette – the
sun, sea, fields and mountains – and our daily
environment can be the inspiration for the colours of
our rugs. In the past, most dyes were derived from
plants or earth pigments, and the colours used in
early rugs reflected their natural origins.

Right: When you dye coloured fabrics you will get quite different
shades from the colours you will achieve with the same dye on
white or natural coloured fabrics. The density and vibrancy of the
colour will depend on many factors, including both the type of dye
and the fibres of which the fabric is made up.

44

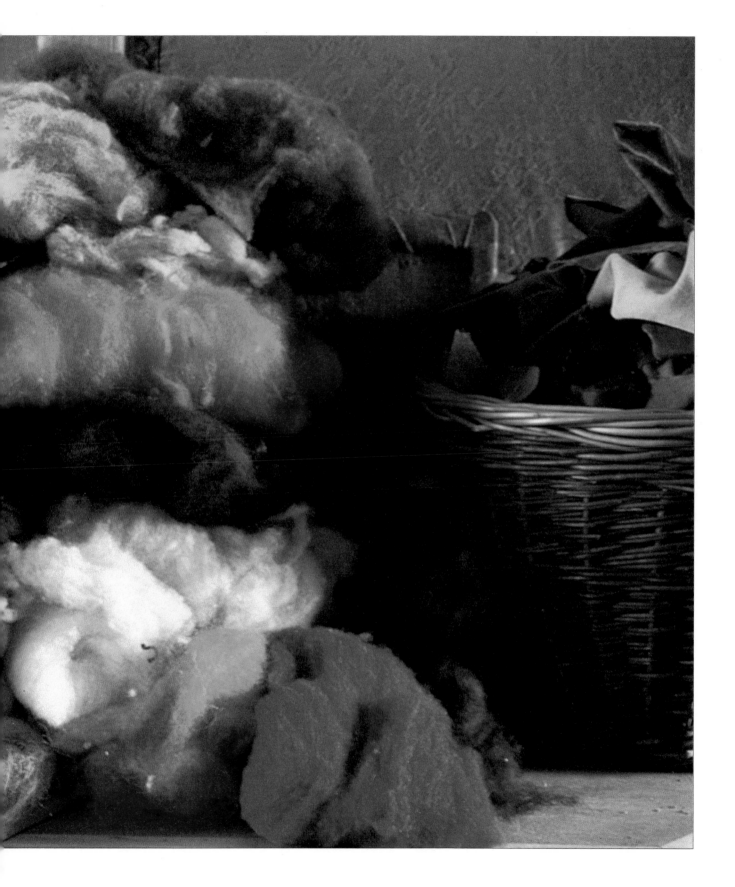

COLOUR ASSOCIATIONS

Yellow is a holy colour in southeast Asia. It is symbolic of purity and dedication in Buddhist communities and is, as a result, the colour of the robes worn by Buddhist monks. In the West it is regarded as a happy, childlike and cheerful colour, having natural associations with sun and warmth. Many people like to decorate their north-facing rooms in shades of yellow as it lifts the spirits and warms the heart.

Orange is yellow's nearest relation, and it, too, is a soft, bright warm colour, reminiscent of early sunsets and glowing fires, which instils a feeling of warmth within us.

Green is the holy colour of Islam throughout the world. It has calm, reverent associations and is linked with nature – leaves, fruit, trees, fields and so on. It is also the colour that, in many cultures, is the symbol of the natural cycle of life and death. For centuries it has been a colour signifying good fortune, although it is also the colour that represents envy, greed and jealousy. It is an 'anchoring colour', as, for example, green foliage holds together the bright tones of flowers and berries. It is, therefore, a good background for a vivid colour scheme.

Blue also has many associations with nature, notably the sky and the sea. Like these, it has an almost infinite quality, depending, of course, on which of its numerous shades is seen. It can be refreshing and serene, restful and expansive. Blues range through the violet-blue of flowers such as bluebells and hyacinths, the turquoise-blue of the ocean, the deep navy of the midnight sky or the azure of a hot summer's day, to the jewel tones of sapphires, lapis lazuli and aquamarines. Although it is often regarded as a cold colour, there are so many different shades and hues that it is possible to find a blue for every mood and occasion.

Red is a hot, passionate colour. When it is included in a colour scheme it becomes the dominant element and demands attention. It is the colour of

Examples of brightly coloured, multi-textured mats made using the hooked and prodded methods.

blood, deadly yet life-enhancing. Red has different associations in different cultures. In much of Asia it is the traditional choice for weddings, and in China New Year celebrations are dominated by the colour, when it signifies happiness and good luck. It is the colour of ripe, sweet fruit and of poisonous berries. It is also the colour of that timeless token of love, the red rose, but it has connotations of rage and is the symbol of danger. The colour is stimulating and signifies action and movement. Because it is difficult to stabilize red as a dye, it was little used in the past and is seen only rarely in early rag rugs.

Colour Theory

Colour is a form of light – that is, the 'colour' of an object is determined by wavelengths in reflected light. For example, there is no yellow in a lemon. If daylight falls on a lemon, the fruit's skin will absorb all the visible wavelengths except yellow, and so we see the lemon as yellow. When an object is white – snow, for example – it absorbs virtually nothing and reflects back most of the wavelengths that fall upon it. A black object, on the other hand, absorbs almost everything and reflects little back. By showing no colour, it produces the visual sensation that we know as black.

The colour we perceive is also affected by the nature of the light. White light, from the sun or an artificial light source, is formed by a combination of all the colours of the spectrum, as was proved by Sir Isaac Newton in 1676. He passed daylight through a prism and broke it down into its components – red, orange, yellow, green, blue, indigo and violet. When he reversed the experiment, by passing these colours back through an inverted prism, they re-combined to produce white light.

These experiments form the foundation of our understanding of colour as it appears in the form of light.

Every colour has its own wavelength, which becomes shorter as we move from red to violet along the spectrum. Therefore red has the longest possible wavelength and violet the shortest possible wavelength. Where the seven main colours mix and blend, more than 200 hues are produced within the spectrum.

Of the seven main colours, three – red, blue and green – cannot be made by mixing light, and these are known as the primary colours. Another attribute of the primary colours is that between them they span the whole of the spectrum because each contains about one-third of all visible wavelengths.

Rag rugs can be made from the humblest of materials, such as shrunken knitwear and faded denim jeans, to the most luxurious of fabrics, including velvet and raw silk. Small amounts of fine fabrics can transform a piece, but remember that they do not wear as well as more everyday material and they are, therefore, best kept for wall-hangings or items such as hats and bags.

Newton showed that if all the colours of the spectrum were combined, the result would be white light, and if red, blue and green were combined the result would, similarly, be white light, provided they were mixed in equal quantities.

Newton went on to prove that if one or more of the seven main colours in the spectrum were missing, the light would not be white but coloured, its hue depending on the colours that remained in the mixture.

When pairs of primary colours are combined in equal amounts, secondary colours are produced. Green and blue make cyan, blue and red make magenta, and red and green make yellow. Varying the balance of the primary colours makes it possible to produce all the colours in the spectrum.

If you look at a colour wheel you will see that each secondary colour appears opposite a primary colour, and these colours are known as complementary – together they make a white light. For example, the secondary colour cyan is a mixture of the primary colours blue and green, which between them account for two-thirds of the visible wavelengths. Opposite cyan on the colour wheel is red, which contains the last third. Cyan and red, therefore, complement each other because when they are mixed in the correct proportions, a white light is produced.

From a designer's point of view, one of the most important aspects of complementary colours is that they represent the greatest possible contrasts. When the colours are used together, they give striking results. Referring to a colour wheel will help you to identify the colours that will work well together in your designs.

Combining Colours

From the colour spectrum and black and white it is possible to produce shades and tints of individual colours. Generally, when colours are darkened they are referred to as shades; when they are lightened they are known as tints.

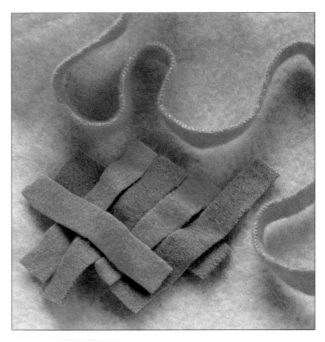

Because it is a natural material and is very fibrous, wool accepts most dyes particularly well. Tones of a single colour will be affected by the mordant that is used and by the length of time that the wool is left in the dye bath.

The soft shades of a length of tartan fabric inspired the browns, pinks and beiges of this batch of dyed wools. Patterned fabrics often give a wonderfully 'textured' look to a rug, and tartans, herringbones and tweeds are especially suitable.

This sampler was hooked in a children's workshop from scraps of unspun and undyed lambs' wool found in hedgerows.
The legs and eyes are worked in a matt black woollen fabric to give a strong contrast.

Fully saturated colours – that is, those that have no black or white added – are naturally brilliant. When these colours are put next to some shades and tints they can lose their vitality and look rather odd. Combining colours that have been altered to the same degree will create a much more harmonious effect.

When you are planning a design, establish the main colour you want to use and work from that. Successful combinations can range from just two colours to fifteen, as long as the colours work together and are pleasing to the eye, which is a subjective decision. There are no strict rules to follow, but remember that you need to get the proportions right – contrasting colours look good, but too much contrast can be overpowering; complementary colours give sharp relief but need to be used with discretion.

The easiest schemes to work with are those in which the colours are closely related but of different strengths. The fewer colours you use, the simpler will be the task of co-ordinating them. When you are designing a rag rug, remember that although contrasting and complementary colours can work very well together, monotones can be just as effective. In fact, for your first attempts, it might be advisable to work with colours from the same family – white, greys and blacks, for example, or blues, ranging from sky to midnight. When you use a simple scheme such as this, the scope for introducing texture is increased and you have more opportunities to use combinations of techniques and materials without having to worry about balancing colours.

The tulip border for a hooked rug, *Sleeping Dog*, by Ali Rhind. Although she dyes many of the fabrics she uses and prepares a detailed rough before she begins, Ali Rhind is never absolutely certain what colour she will use next, which gives her work a freshness and spontaneity.

Once you feel comfortable with the techniques, you can begin to experiment with colours. The colour wheel and colour theory will help you to understand the science of colour, but the selection of colour is always subjective, and you should never allow theory to outweigh your personal preference.

If the design of your rug is a largely pictorial one – a butterfly, flower or cat, for example – a simple, solid colour as background will probably be ideal. Such a background will set off the colours in the main area of your design. If you are working on an abstract design, however, you may want to use an array of colours to emphasize textural details.

Bear in mind, too, that contrast plays an important part of any design, with dark backgrounds offsetting vibrant, colourful motifs and vice versa.

Some writers recommend that when it comes to placing colour it is wisest to stick to tried and tested combinations. If you do this you can be sure of making no mistakes, and the reactions of others to your work will probably be favourable and unsurprised.

You may, however, prefer to be more adventurous. You may understand about the science of colour and which colours, theoretically, should be used together, but you may decide to make your selection on purely personal grounds. Other people's reactions to your choice may range from the enthusiastic to the discouraging, but if you are making something that you are going to live with, the colours must be your choice. If you are happy with the colour scheme, use it.

Colour and Texture

Most homes contain items of furniture, but the elements that infuse a home with personality and warmth are the accessories and colour. The accessories are usually the soft furnishings – upholstery, cushions, carpets, curtains and rugs – and textiles have been used as furnishing accessories for centuries, from earliest times being used to add luxury, comfort and decoration to hard furniture, walls and floors. No matter what the texture of the fabrics, they will always soften the appearance of a room because fabrics are almost always tactile.

Working with colour on textiles differs from working with colour on other media. The fibres and fabrics, the rags and scraps you choose for your rag rugs, have their own individual textures and qualities, and they catch and reflect light in very different ways from flat media. Colour charts, illustrations in magazines, paintings and so on can be useful in your initial selection process, but the various fabrics you use will look quite different when they are placed next to each other.

Consider the ways in which fibres and colours affect each other when they are placed side by side. Look at the way a rough texture appears when it is juxtaposed with a smooth texture; place the same fabric next to a piece of material with a shiny finish and one with a dull finish. The colour of the fabric will appear to change when it is placed next to different textures, and part of the joy of working with combinations of materials is that they are never predictable or constant.

When they were originally made, rag rugs were, literally, made from rags – the fabrics used were often dull and aged, their colours were faded and the material was thin. Today, however, we have a wide selection not only of comparatively inexpensive, new fabrics to choose from but also a variety of synthetic, easy-to-use dyes, which makes it relatively easy to change the colour of the fabrics we use. Before you use any dye, however, bear in mind that different

Charity (thrift) shops and car boot and jumble sales are excellent sources of materials. Do not simply look out for the obvious fabrics – many rag rug makers incorporate plastics, rubber and many kinds of synthetic materials in their work.

The range of tones and shades of a single colour can be spectacular, and these can be further enhanced, as here, when the different textures of silk, taffeta and velour are used. A rug worked in a single colour but a variety of fabrics can look wonderfully varied.

Ideas for designs and colours can come from all kinds of sources, from the flowers in the garden to feathers found
on the ground as you walk through the countryside. If you are working on a pictorial design, it is sometimes a good idea
to prepare several sketches so that you can develop your ideas.

fabrics and fibres accept dyes in different ways, and a variety of tones and shades will result, depending on the coarseness or smoothness of the fabric fibres.

Experiment for yourself by wrapping a thick, coarse yarn around a piece of card. Illuminate it from one side only, so that each strand of yarn is partly in the light and partly in the shade, then move the card so that the light falls on the yarn from different angles. Notice how the tones change as the yarns moves out of and into shadow. Repeat the experiment with a fine, smooth yarn, and you will see that the differences in tone between the shaded and illuminated areas are less because the surface of the fibre is more regular than that of the coarse yarn.

When you dye yarns you must consider how much the texture of a fibre can affect its apparent colour. Smooth fibres, such as silk and nylon, reflect light, giving the fabric a lustre and brightness. Cotton, wool and flax, which are either hairy or have been artificially flattened, have irregular surfaces that absorb more light and that appear duller and darker. If a piece of wool and a piece of silk that had been dyed exactly the same colour were placed side by side, the silk would appear to be brighter than the wool.

Selecting colours for your rug, therefore, involves considering the texture of the fabric as well as its shade.

DYEING

If you are keen to change the colour of the fabrics you are planning to use for your rag rugs, you will probably consider using a dye of some kind. As a craft in its own right, dyeing is very rewarding, and to dye fabrics for your own rag rug would make it doubly satisfying. You can transform old fabrics into rich, beautifully coloured scraps that will help you create an entirely original piece of work. Whether you use natural or synthetic dyes is up to you, but it does depend on the kind of effect you want to achieve.

Chemical dyes have been a great advantage to the rag rug maker, making it possible to alter the colours of the fabrics you have without having to seek out expensive or time-consuming means of doing so. It is, however, possible to use natural dyes, either proprietary mixes, which are becoming increasingly available, or ones that you prepare yourself from plants.

Designed for the Canadian High Commission in London, *Souvenir* now hangs in the office of the Cultural Attaché. The hooked work includes the motif of a maple leaf, which is an instantly recognizable symbol of Canada, as well as a variety of other references to traditional Canadian culture.

Types of Dye

For thousands of years colours used for dyeing were obtained from natural sources – animals, vegetables and minerals. Egyptians of the Middle Kingdom (2000 bc) knew how to apply madder and weld as dyes, and the reds, oranges and terracottas they produced have lasted to this day. Indigo was used in Japan as long ago as the seventh century, and the Mexicans used cochineal to create a red dye before the conquistadores arrived.

In Europe before the industrial revolution of the nineteenth century the use of natural dyes was very limited, and colours derived from single sources would vary widely from batch to batch. It was only when spun and woven yarns began to be mass-produced that it became important that shades matched and that fashionable colours could be produced and reproduced accurately.

Aniline Dyes

The dyeing industry struggled to keep abreast of the cotton industry until 1856, when a student at the Royal College of Chemistry in London, William Henry Perkin (1838–1907), was conducting experiments with coal tar to try to develop a synthetic quinine. Perkin discovered a synthetic purple dye, and the colour is now known as Perkin's violet in his memory. Purple was a difficult colour to achieve with natural dyes – the difficulty and expense being reflected in the fact that it has been regarded as an imperial or regal colour since Roman times. Perkin immediately realized the potential of his discovery and set about exploiting it commercially.

The revelation that colour could be produced in the laboratory led to further research throughout Europe. In 1868 two German chemists, Karl Graebe and Carl Liebermann, discovered how to synthesize the natural dye alizarin from anthraquinone. (Alizarin is the compound found in the madder plant that

This contoured chain stitch rug is worked in an array of bright, intense hues. If you cannot find suitably coloured fabrics then dyeing is the answer. The fabric used came from old T-shirts, cut into narrow strips, and this has the great advantage that it rolls itself into pliable cord when it is cut.

produces its red and brown colouring effects.) From this discovery it was established that synthetic dyes could be produced that were both strong and stable, and it led to the development of synthetic magenta, blues, violets, greens and reds before the end of the century.

These new colours were based on a derivative of coal tar called aniline. Aniline made it possible to control the strength of the dye and the purity of the colour, so that it was easier to match colours and reduce the cost of the production process. However, although aniline dyes produce brilliant colours on natural fibres, they are not fast and do not hold their colour. The solution to this problem that was adopted in the 1860s was 'mordanting'. Mordants fix colours, acting as chemical bridges, and they can be found in natural dyes as well as produced synthetically. Natural dyes can be either substantive (which need no mordant) or adjective (which have no direct affinity with the textile fabric and therefore require a mordant). A mordant that is used with adjective dyes is a metallic salt that is added during the dyeing process to improve the fastness of the colour by encouraging an affinity between the dye and the fibres. Adding a chromium salt during the dyeing will improve colour fastness even more. Other mordants are iron, tin, salt, vinegar and caustic soda.

Acid Dyes

Experiments to synthesize the dye elements occurring in natural dyestuffs led in 1875 to the discovery of acid dyes. These dyes were found to work well in a water solution with wool, silk and fabrics with hairy fibres. If it is to produce a fast, bright colour, an acid dye has to be processed in acidic conditions – a hot, acidulated dye bath with vinegar (not salt) used as a mordant.

Disperse Dyes

In 1923 a method of dyeing acetate rayon was discovered. The fibres of this fabric could not be

According to the old adage, 'red and green should never be seen'. But these shades look so striking together that it is difficult to resist combining them. When you are dyeing fabrics, try leaving pieces in the dye bath for different times so that you build up a selection of subtly graded shades.

dyed by any of the existing methods because no dyestuff could be dissolved to produce a solution that was compatible with rayon. The dyes are named because they disperse into water rather than dissolving in it. They have to be used with a special agent that keeps the dye evenly distributed in the dye bath because the particles would otherwise tend to sink to the bottom. Disperse dyes can be used on all types of synthetic fabrics – acetate, acrylic, nylon and polyester – but you need to check that the dye you use is specifically designed to be compatible with the type of fabric.

Direct Dyes

Although these dyes are simple to use they fade quickly when they are washed. This kind of dye is most suitable for fabrics that are not going to be washed frequently – curtains, rugs and wall-hangings, for example – and they are, therefore, ideal for fabrics to be used in rag rugs.

Fibre-reactive Dyes

A range of dyes has been developed to form a stronger, more permanent bond between the colour and the fabric. These dyes are brilliant and clear and are suitable for viscose, rayon, silk, linen, cotton and other plant fibres, but the range of colours is not as wide as that of acid dyes. Dyeing can be carried out in hot or cold water, depending on the kind of dye that is used, and salt is added to encourage the dye to bond with the fibres.

Domestic cold-water dyes, such as those produced by Dylon, are known as cold-water

Natural dyes give a range of natural colours, mostly in the red, brown and yellow range, while synthetic dyes range from bright, clear colours to more sedate shades. You can also obtain excellent dyes that can be used in the washing machine.

reactive dyes. The difference between cold-water dyes and conventional dyes is that conventional dyes are sold in a range of basic colours that permits flexibility about mixing colours. Cold-water dyes are sold as pre-mixed colours and do not mix well.

Natural Dyes

The development of synthetic dyestuffs has meant that natural dyes have gradually fallen from use. In the past few years, however, interest in natural dyes has shown signs of reviving, and it would be wholly appropriate to use natural dyes to colour the fabrics to be used in a rag rug. You will find potential material in your garden and in the countryside – leaves and stems, flower heads, roots, berries and seeds, onion skins can all be used. Almost every plant will give some colour, usually in the yellow to brown range, and this can be modified by the use of a different mordant. This is too large a topic to be covered here, but if you are interested you will find it a rewarding and fascinating subject.

Using Dyes

Before you begin to use a dye of any kind, you must observe a few basic safety guidelines:

- Completely clear your work area and cover surfaces with newspaper to protect them from accidental spills.
- Make sure that you are working in a well-ventilated room.
- Make sure that all equipment is clearly labelled and is used only for dyeing.
- Wear rubber gloves to protect your hands. It is also a good idea to wear old clothes or an apron.
- When you handle dye powders, wear a face mask so that you do not inhale any dust.

Equipment

You will probably already find most of the equipment you will need in your home. However, do remember that you should keep the items separate from the other things in your kitchen and never use the implements you have used for dyeing for cooking.

- *Dye pots* must be heatproof and non-reactive. Glass and enamel are suitable, but stainless steel is probably best because it will not stain, is unbreakable and is inert. Use an old saucepan that is large enough to contain the fibre or fabric at boiling temperatures without boiling over.

- *Measuring and weighing implements* will be needed to measure dye powders, stocks and fabrics. Graduated plastic beakers are useful for small amounts of dye stock, but measuring spoons will give more accurate results for smaller amounts. You can obtain sets of measuring spoons, ranging from 1.25ml to 20ml (1/4 tsp to 1 tbsp), from some chemists and from good cookware shops. You will also need a heatproof, 1l (1 1/4 pt) measuring jug for dye solutions and some bathroom or kitchen scales for weighing fabrics.

- *Stirring rods* are needed for mixing solutions, for stirring and manipulating hot, wet fabrics and for transferring fabrics from one pot to another. Heatproof glass rods do not stain, but you could use chopsticks or wooden or plastic mixing spoons. If you use wood, which will stain, and intend to do a lot of dyeing, consider keeping a selection for different colours so there is no risk of colour being transferred.

- You will need a *heat source* to boil dye solutions. Your domestic gas or electric cooker is probably more than adequate.

- Keep a *selection of bottles* to store solutions and chemicals. Plastic is lighter and safer than glass. Label all storage jars.

Finally, you should keep a notebook in which you record the results of all your experiments. Note not only the type of dye and the type of material but also the time taken and the number of times the fabric was placed in the dye bath.

Natural yarns or woollen materials, such as blankets, look amazing in their undyed state, but they also accept dyes very well. Use dyed and undyed fabrics together with printed and painted materials to achieve richness of tone and depth of colour. Lay different textures next to each other before rejecting anything.

Preparing Fabric for Dyeing

If you are using old garments, cut off the hems, seams and selvage edges before dyeing. Wash the fabric by hand in hot water or in the moderate/ medium cycle of your machine to remove any dressing the manufacturer has used and to clean the fabric so that the dye will take evenly.

If you are using old items of knitwear, you may want to felt the woollen garments first. Wash them in the hot cycle of your machine at a temperature that will shrink the garments and make them fluffy and felt-like.

Tear or cut the washed fabrics into appropriately sized pieces for your rugging purposes. This will make them easier to handle during the dyeing process, too.

Unexpected combinations of colours can sometimes be effective. These green rag strips on an orange background are almost the colour of delicious tagliatelle. When it comes to combining colours, the only rule to remember is that there is no rule. Be adventurous.

Dyeing Fabrics

Fibre-reactive dyes and acid dyes are suitable for rugs and hangings. These are, in fact, the dyes used in the industry for the manufacture of carpets and dress fabrics. They are usually supplied in powder or granule form, which mix easily with water to form the dye stock. Because these dyes need an acid assistant, vinegar is added to the dye bath to fix the colour. The simplest way to estimate the amount of vinegar you will need is to weigh the fabric and halve that figure – for example, for every 50g (2oz) of fabric you will need 25ml (1fl oz) of vinegar.

The following quantities will make 1l (1½pt) of stock solution, which is sufficient for about 1kg (2¼lb) weight of fabric.

- Put about 10ml (2 tsp) of the dye powder into a measuring jug and add 1–2 drops of washing-up liquid.
- Add a tiny amount of boiling water and mix to a paste.

- Gradually add about 1l (1½pt) of hot water to make up the required amount. Stir continually while you add the water.
- Allow the dye to cool, then pour into a bottle to store. Label the bottle clearly.

Once the dye stock solution has been prepared, you are ready to proceed with the dyeing. The instructions and methods described below are specifically designed for dyeing rags for the purposes of making rugs. If you are dyeing rags, they will probably not be white, so it is a good idea to dye a small piece of white cloth before you begin so that you can see the true colour of the dye.

Dyeing Recycled Knitwear

Collect together about 200g (8oz) of woollen fabrics. Fill a bucket with warm water and add a couple of drops of washing-up liquid. Mix the water and detergent thoroughly, then add the fabrics and leave them to soak for 1 hour. Prepare the dye bath, making up a solution of dye stock, vinegar and water as follows:

- *Water:* 30 x fabric weight – that is, if you have 200g (8oz) of fabric you will need 6000ml/6l (240fl oz/12pt).
- *Vinegar:* half the fabric weight – that is, 200g (8oz) of fabric requires 100ml (4fl oz).
- *Dye stock solution:* for a pale solution use the equivalent of half the weight of the fabric, for a medium solution use the equivalent weight of the fabric and for a dark solution use double the equivalent weight of the fabric – that is, for a medium dye for 200g (8oz) of fabric use 200ml (8fl oz) of dye solution.

Mix the dye stock, vinegar and water together.

Squeeze the water from the fabric that has been soaking in the bucket, separate the pieces and place them in the dye bath. Push the fabric down into the water quickly to make sure that every piece is evenly covered. Slowly heat the dye bath to simmering point, which can take 30–45 minutes, stirring the fabrics with a rod or spoon every 5–10 minutes.

Keep the dye bath at simmering point for a further 30–45 minutes, stirring occasionally. Do not try to rush this process. Turn off the heat and allow the contents of the dye bath to cool.

Rinse the fabric in cool water until the water runs clear. Spin in the washing machine or roll in towels until the pieces are dry.

The dye solution left in the dye bath is of no further use. Dilute it even further and dispose of it down an outside drain.

Place the onion skins and 1litre (1½pt) of water in the dye bath. Bring this to a simmer and leave at this temperature for about 45 minutes. Allow to cool and then strain into a clean container. Discard the onion skins and rinse out the dye bath.

To 2.5l (5pt) of water add 50ml (1½fl oz) of vinegar and the dye liquor stock. Stir well.

Squeeze out the surplus water from the soaked fabric, separate the pieces and place them in the dye bath with the water, vinegar and dye stock. Slowly bring the solution to simmering point, which should take about 30 minutes, then simmer for a further 40 minutes, stirring the mixture from time to time.

Leave the dye to cool, remove the fabric from the dye bath and rinse it until the water runs clear.

Natural Dyes

There are two main ways of extracting colour from natural dyestuffs. Materials such as leaves, petals or stems must be boiled, as described above for onion skins. Some natural dyestuffs – henna and cutch (catechu), for example – are supplied as powders, however. To extract colour from these, it is necessary to mix the powder into a paste with some cold water, gradually adding more water until you have sufficient for the dye bath. Once you have dyed the fabric, it is essential to rinse it thoroughly to remove any remaining particles of powder. Some powders – logwood extract, for example – will dissolve completely in hot water. When you use a powder, bear in mind that the extracts give a much stronger colour than the ones that can be obtained from petals, leaves and stems, so you will need to use less.

The colours from two of the oldest natural dyes – indigo and madder – are created by neither of these methods, however.

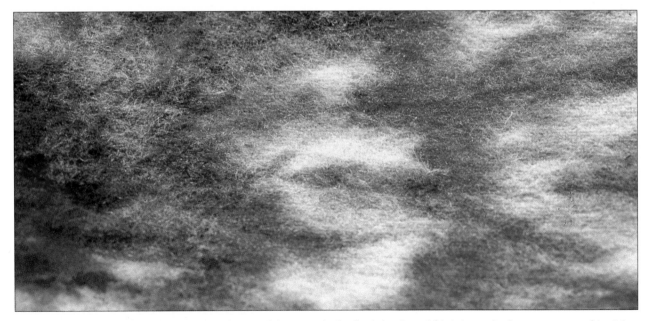

Unusual results are possible with tie dyeing and textured dyeing methods. If a dark coloured fabric is overdyed, you may succeed in giving it extra depth. Mixing different coloured fleeces together and then felting them can produce unexpectedly lovely results.

DESIGN AND INSPIRATIONS

Once you have chosen the materials, textures and colours you want to use, the next consideration is the actual design.

When you are faced with a blank piece of hessian, you may be overwhelmed by the thought that you can portray almost anything you want to. There are so many sources of inspiration – from the piece of fruit you eat for breakfast to the pillowcase into which you snuggle at night – that it can be difficult to know where to start.

Begin with some research in art galleries, museums, book shops and markets. Developing an awareness of movements in art and trends in interior design will help you to be alert to new ideas and will help to catalyse and encourage any thoughts you may already have. Train yourself to think about what you see rather than merely looking at objects that you normally take for granted. You will learn to look at colours, textures, shapes and images in a new way when you look at them as potential design sources.

Old rag rugs may inspire you to create traditional-looking patterns, although the variety of sizes, patterns and designs is so great that there is no particular 'traditional' style to follow, although some themes have always been popular.

As we have seen, many early rugs were rectangular because feed sacks were often used as the base fabric, and the size of the sacks determined the size and, to some extent the shape, of the finished rugs.

Right: This detail of Juju Vail's *This is the home and native land where my world began* shows the neat hooking technique. It also shows how clear plastic carrier bags have been worked into the rug to create the impression of flakes of snow.

Ali Rhind develops her ideas in a series of sketches, and she keeps strips of dyed wool and initial colour ideas together. The blues and greens have been dyed to match the feathers, and the natural dyes used give the fabrics a real intensity of colour.

Some ambitious makers would stitch several rugs together to make stair runs and room-sized floor-coverings. Today, with hessian available on rolls, your rug can be almost any size you wish, but you might want to consider where it will be placed in the home, the length of time you are prepared to spend working on it and the kind of design you want to work.

So many early rugs were used until they became threadbare that we have only a few examples of early motifs – domestic animals, seaside scenes and children. The introduction of stencilled rug patterns by Edward Sands Frost in the mid-nineteenth century increased the popularity of hooking but at the same time reduced the range of home-designed patterns. Spurred on by the success of Frost's pre-printed patterns, other makers began to supply ready-printed designs, which began to become more formal and symmetrical. After about 1875 the pre-printed designs often included indications of the colours that should be used, and this led to a certain degree of uniformity among many of the rugs made in the latter part of the century. Nevertheless, although the patterns were very popular, many rug makers used the pre-printed design only as a starting point, introducing their own colours and quirks as they worked.

It is possible to find pre-printed designs in some specialist shops. However, the enormous amount of visual material that surrounds us these days, together with such designs aids as tracing paper and photocopiers, means that it is possible to have almost any image you want on your rug, from a comic character to the Mona Lisa.

The rugs described in the next chapter will give you some idea of the scope that is available to you, but some of the main themes are briefly discussed here.

GEOMETRIC DESIGNS

Beginners used to work geometric designs in order to practise the craft of hooking, for no drawing skills are required to mark off a geometric pattern. As they gained experienced, the makers could develop the designs into complex repeating patterns. Quilt and patchwork designs were often the inspiration for rugs, and simple motifs, such as hearts, stars and moons, were included in many geometric patterns or incorporated in borders.

Because many of the geometrically patterned rag rugs were made by beginners for practice purposes, they were never given pride of place in the home. Many were put next to the sink or stove or used as doormats. Such rugs were worn by constant use and are now keenly sought after by collectors.

HIT AND MISS RUGS

Scraps of fabric from existing rag rugs would be saved and carefully wound into balls. These scraps were then often woven, either at home or by the local weaver, into woven rag rugs. If these scraps were incorporated into a hooked rug, they gave an uneven texture to the finished rug – a 'hit and miss' texture. The scraps were also sometimes hooked into new rugs in a haphazard, chaotic pattern.

ABSTRACT DESIGNS

In order to make a rag rug it is necessary to collect sufficient rags and scraps of material to finish a design. When a specific pattern has been worked, the thrifty rag rug maker may keep the mixture of fabrics left over and then use all the bits and pieces to make

From a series of initial sketches, Ali Rhind builds up her design ideas, working them up in colour with designer's gouache paints. She prefers simple patterns and strong colours, and when she is happy with the design, she dyes fabrics to match her coloured sketches.

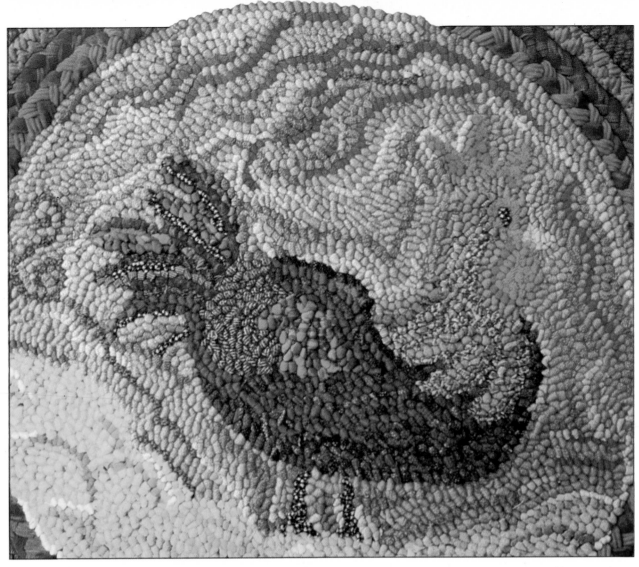

Margaret Docherty uses several techniques in her rugs, and she often draws her inspiration from the things she sees around her every day.
This rug was inspired by the cockerel that lives in the farmyard below her studio.

an abstract design. There is no set definition of what is 'abstract', so you can create any patterns of lines, circles, squiggles and so on that appeals to you. The only limitation might be that the colours and design are balanced within the available space.

DOMESTIC SCENES

Many of the early North American rag rugs portray motifs and scenes that were familiar in the everyday life of the people who made them – their gardens, homes and neighbours. Some of the scenes that were shown in rag rugs were very realistic, while others were childlike and primitive in the manner in which they were drawn and in the use of perspective.

The objects and people that were shown provide us with a glimpse of the world of the people who made the rugs, as little details of their lives were recorded. Cats were always popular subjects. The guardian of the hearth, the family cat would often be portrayed in rugs to be placed in front of the fire. Sentimental rag rug hookers tended to depict objects, people or animals that were dear to their hearts or to record the dates of special occasions. Other rag rugs, known today as spite rugs, depicted mocking or scornful images of unfaithful husbands or disliked relatives.

Today, these homely but unique images are among the most highly valued of all rag rugs.

Cushion pads are a traditional way of making hard chairs a little more comfortable. The design of the pad in the background was inspired by Hausa motifs, and the pad is part of the stool itself. The pad in the foreground is made by braiding.

FLOWERS AND FRUIT

Throughout the late nineteenth century, in both Britain and North America, floral motifs were popular in all kinds of interior decoration, including furniture upholstery, wallpapers and ornamental motifs on fireplaces and walls. Floral hooked rugs were made to mark special occasions, ranging from christenings to funerals. In winter, when fresh flowers were not available, a floral rag rug was draped over the coffin, and these are now known as coffin rugs.

Bouquets and garlands were often combined with fruits, and some especially elaborate designs in this style were made by the French settlers in Nova Scotia and Acadia, who copied them from the rich textiles of their homeland. These French-inspired patterns often include bouquets with central floral motifs worked in soft pinks, violets and mauves with an ivory-coloured background. Rag rugs with floral motifs from New England tended to be worked with brown or tan-coloured backgrounds to match the pinewood floors found in most homes.

Floral rag rugs with white backgrounds are most keenly sought after by collectors today; they are very rare and particularly treasured.

ORIENTAL CARPETS

Almost everyone who works with textiles finds inspiration in the wonderful designs of Oriental rugs and carpets. In the United States after the Civil War (1861–5) the homes of the newly prosperous were filled with finery, including imported, hand-knotted carpets from the East. Many could not afford such luxurious pieces, however, but the carpets were a rich source of inspiration for home rug hookers, and Edward Sands Frost's company even supplied a range of Turkish, Oriental and Persian pre-stencilled designs.

To achieve colours that were as similar as possible to Oriental rugs, pieces of woollen fabric were dyed terracotta, earth brown, ivory and other mellow shades, and the pieces were hooked into intricate

patterns. A velvet sheen was given by clipping off the tops of the hooked loops. Many home rug hookers, however, chose not to use the traditional colours – with surprising results.

These samplers were made for a workshop at which Ali Rhind demonstrated the two basic rug making techniques –
hooking and prodding. Both pieces are called *Daffodils in a Jug*, and although they were worked on the same background, they reveal
very clearly the differences in texture and overall effect that the two techniques produce.

FROM INITIAL DESIGN TO COMPLETED WORK

Juju Vail works out her initial ideas for colours and motifs, and she often uses a computer to help her manipulate shapes and colours. After this process she takes a print, on which she can experiment still further.

When she is satisfied with her initial sketches, Juju Vail takes the design one stage further by making a collage of paper, which she stitches together to give her an idea of how the finished rug will look. She can easily change the colours at this stage and even add threads or fabrics and it is a simple task to dismantle and reassemble the elements in a different way.

This is the final artwork for Juju Vail's *This is the home and native land where my world began*, which was designed to express her feelings about Canada and her roots in that country. The finished rug follows this design closely in terms of pattern, colour and texture.

The finished version of Juju Vail's *This is the home and native land where my world began*, which incorporates recycled materials and fabrics picked up in charity (thrift) shops and jumble sales. The sparkling details are worked in strips cut from plastic carrier bags.

DESIGNERS
AT WORK

✳

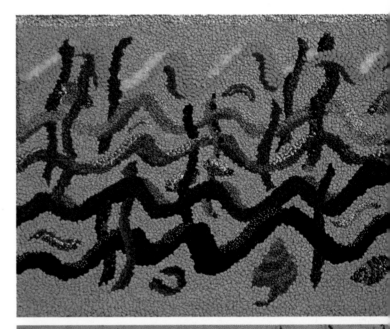

On the following pages the work of some of today's most innovative and talented rag rug makers is illustrated and discussed. The artists explain how and why they were attracted to rag rug making, and they describe their working methods and their sources of inspiration.

Making rag rugs is an intrinsic part of the life of each of the designers featured here. This chapter focuses on the motivation of the artists and what inspires their creativity. Not all the makers work exclusively in this medium. Most, often for economic reasons, integrate rag rug making with other areas of their working lives. The one uniting factor of the artists featured is that they have chosen an historically utilitarian craft as their preferred medium. Today rag rug making is no longer regarded simply as the making of functional items. It is a language adopted by artists to express an idea or belief or to challenge and re-define preconceptions of traditions. The way in which they approach their work, their methods of working and the results are as individual as the artists themselves.

PRUE BRAMWELL-DAVIS

Prue Bramwell-Davis went to art school twice. In the 1960s she trained as an industrial designer, and in the 1980s she undertook a part-time course in constructed textiles from a craft perspective. This second course was ostensibly about the development of materials and technologies and about the processes involved, but it also required the students to develop their own repertoire of media and techniques. During the course, Prue went on a one-day rag rugging workshop run by Jeannie Bates, and on that day she began work on a rug that became the first in a series of war rugs. She was struck by the potential of rag rug making from that very day.

Prue loves drawing, and she also paints and is a keen photographer. She enjoys the processes of visual research and development and happily spends the time between identifying initial subjects of interest – the visual exploration and development on a page or a series of small experiments – and the crystallization of the ideas into a finished design. As in all work with a medium like rag rugging, discoveries occur during the process of actually making the piece, and Prue finds this flexibility one of the most rewarding, and challenging.

Her initial inspiration came from traditional rugs, but she did not feel constrained to continue to work within the confines of the tradition nor to work merely with the traditional materials and techniques. She is always diversifying the materials she uses, and she says that she 'continues to break up the matrix as well as the surface of the rug itself as a sort of parallel metaphor to the development of the original idea'.

She does not see herself as being influenced by design, pattern or format. Her work is about 'ideas that may be suitable for treatment through the medium of rag rugging'. She identifies two areas of focus. 'The first operates at the surface and is to do with visual wit and intrigue. The second is below the surface and aims to use rag rug making to explore political ideas..Sometimes the two territories overlap. I have found that there is such a power of attraction in the physical presence of the "rug" – the consciousness of the choices of materials and the progress of every step almost shout out at the viewer – that the medium is immensely powerful, and I find it draws ideas out of me.'

Prue confesses that rag rug making is not a thrifty way of creating textiles! It does, however, fit in well with broader concerns that she has about the pressures that the crafts establishment exerts on the consumer culture. She feels that there is a constant emphasis on the creative, almost fine art aspects of non-industrially produced objects, which are marketed as commodities in exactly the same way as mass-produced objects by being advertised as having special qualities that are, nevertheless, available to all. The more subtle and interesting subject of the pleasure of making, which is not, of course, of interest in a discourse concerned only with selling, has, she feels, been completely sidelined.

'From what I have observed and read,' she says, 'many craftspeople (who have the economic option) are much more interested in the process of making than in striving to be creative in an innovatory sense. ... Any maker is familiar with the fact that a great deal of creative decision-making happens at the point of meeting of the tool and the working surface, and that is more than enough. Rag rug making, when it was little more than a clever way to get a carpet from clothes, was, I think, more about this modest perspective, and I like that as a starting point. What I absolutely abhor is the forcing of the home-made

A designer by training, Prue Bramwell-Davies carries a sketchbook with her in which she notes shapes and textures and plays around with them to create new designs. This hooked wall-hanging, *Between the Lines*, was the result of just such a process.

object, with the additional quality of "exotic", into the market economy through the slavery of children in parts of the world where there is no opportunity of having the choice of making something for the sheer pleasure of making.'

Prue uses whatever materials and techniques she needs to achieve the effects she wants, and she does not feel at all inhibited by traditional media. The fact that pieces are not made for the floor has helped her to separate the traditional craft from the technique. When it is necessary, she dyes fabrics, using either synthetic or natural dyes, because she uses dyed fabrics in her other textile work, but otherwise she relies on new fabrics or cast-off clothes from her family. She sometimes uses a frame, but not always – she trades practicality against portability.

She has not sold much of her work, but is happy to let the purely visual pieces go. Prue wants the more political pieces to communicate on a broad front, so she is careful where they go. She exhibits, partly through Fibreworks, a group of textile artists, which holds at least one exhibition yearly in London.

BARBARA CARROLL

Barbara Carroll started hooking rugs with Emma Lou Lais in Kansas City, Missouri, in 1987. In 1993 she moved to Ligonier in Pennsylvania and began to offer bed-and-breakfast accommodation in her cottage. It was from here that she began to run workshops teaching the art of rug hooking in the primitive style. Every May she runs a special workshop, lasting for five days, in which students are able to develop their skills in rag rug hooking with the help of experienced rag rug teachers. Barbara describes her own work as: 'Whimsical thoughts that come about with great wools, warm muffins and hot tea.'

Below: The charming image of a man driving a pig to market is in the North American tradition. The hand hooking technique that Barbara Carroll uses lends itself very well to this naïve style, which could well be an illustration for a nursery rhyme or fairy tale. Note how the star and moon blend into the background.

The American rag rug tradition is reflected in this hand hooked rug, which Barbara Carroll made with recycled woollen materials.

Dogs have always been popular subjects for rag rug hookers, and Barbara Carroll has chosen
to depict a Scottie dog and its kennel on this hand hooked rug.

LOUISA CREED

Although she makes the most charming cats and landscapes, Louisa Creed is a flautist, not an artist. She has been making rag rugs and wall-hangings for only about eight years. She first saw some rag rugs at the Rufus Craft Centre in Nottingham and was immediately inspired to make one herself. She had no idea how to make a rag rug and is entirely self-taught. She believes that she makes them in a slightly unorthodox way.

She is sometimes inspired to design a rug by a photograph or a postcard, sometimes by a landscape. She approaches hooking a rug more as an artist than as a craftswoman, and she spends a great deal of time painstakingly working out the designs. Although colour is a great motivation, the greatest thrill, she says, is seeing a cat emerge from the hessian.

Her work is so neat that it comes as something of a surprise to learn that she works without a frame, holding the hessian on her lap. She works as a means of relaxation after a busy day of music. Her materials come mainly from jumble sales, and she does not dye her fabrics. She likes to use a lot of close tones, positioning them near to each other. In a sky, for example, she may use up to 15 shades of blue. She will use any kind of material as long as it is the right colour. She hems the hessian before she begins work, and hooks right up to the edge.

Right: In *Rosie in the Airing Cupboard* Louisa Creed has captured perfectly the expression of a rather elderly cat who has been disturbed during its favourite occupation – dozing in a warm place. The horizontal lines of the neatly folded laundry create patterns around the cat.

This dramatic image was worked by the hooked method. A huge range of colours was used to complete *Black Puss*, and the shades have been skilfully deployed to convey the movement and texture of the cat's fur.

She doesn't cover the back of her work because she believes that dust gets trapped inside.

She does not like parting with her work and has sold only one piece – to a friend. However, she may be persuaded to sell in the future when her collection of pieces is larger.

Right: The eyes of this enormous cat seem to follow the watcher around the room. *Oswald* is in a typical feline pose, ready to pounce on an unsuspecting passer-by.

Below: Louisa Creed designed *Rosie on a Ben Nicholson Cushion* to have three distinct elements. The curled-up form of the life-like cat sinks into the cushion. The cushion itself is decorated with stylized animals, which are shown in silhouette and are quite stiff compared with the smooth curves of the cat, while the background to the cushion forms a third, contrasting section.

Above: The Baltimore Quilt by Ann Davies is one of the most finely textured rugs illustrated in this book. The rug, which is worked in woollen fabrics, is based on the traditional American patchwork quilt. To give it an antique look, it was dyed in tea.

Opposite: The use of fine, closely woven wool, cut into very fine strips, makes it possible to introduce greater detail than is possible with more coarsely hooked rugs. This cornucopia, a detail of the Baltimore Quilt, is very pretty and could be worked on its own as a sampler.

ANN DAVIES

Ann Davies is the founder of the Rag Rug Society of the UK, which now has 120 members.

She had always been interested in textile crafts, but her interest in rag rugs began in the mid-1960s, when she attended a textile course at Goldsmith's College in London.

'While we were there,' she remembers, 'we were encouraged to experiment, and I recalled reading an article in an American magazine when I had lived in Singapore. I really thought that rag rug making was a North American craft, and it was only after extensive research that I was able to find out more about it. By trial and error I came to incorporate rag rug techniques into my textiles, and [I] became more and more involved in rag rug making and less and less in embroidery.'

Ann takes much of her inspiration from stained glass windows, although almost anything can set off ideas for a design – sometimes a material, sometimes an exhibition she has visited. She is currently interested in extending her designs through computer-aided design packages.

Ann's inspiration for the Baltimore Quilt was an American appliqué quilt. It is very beautiful and so finely made that it could almost be a blanket. The background rags were dyed in tea to give them an aged appearance, which contrasts well with the bright red and green of the design.

Because her work is very fine and therefore time consuming to complete, she sells little, although examples are in collections in both the UK and the United States. She prefers to work to her own designs rather than working on commissions, although she is happy to sell her completed work.

Ann teaches all over the UK, mostly at adult education centres. She also runs occasional weekend courses at Missenden Abbey, Buckinghamshire. She is brilliant at demonstrating a whole range of rug techniques and at encouraging and promoting newcomers to the craft.

MARGARET DOCHERTY

A passion for all things to do with textiles, especially Turkish rugs, led Margaret Docherty to rag rug making. In the 1960s and 1970s she travelled widely in Turkey, and she was intrigued by the large frames used for carpet weaving that she saw in many Turkish homes, where they took up almost all the communal living space. Margaret has also lived in Kenya, where she learned about dyeing fabrics, and she has also studied pottery and hat making.

Margaret Docherty is shown working on a prodded rug in the countryside that provides so much inspiration for her rugs and hangings.

Although born in Edinburgh, Margaret now lives in a small town in the southwest of England, and she finds inspiration in the hens, geese, ducks, water-wheel and stream that she sees in the countryside around her. She has also been influenced by the countries and crafts she has seen. Hausa embroidery, for example, was the inspiration behind her chain stitch pieces. Many of her recent works include sheep and cockerels, but she also admires Indian embroidery.

At present, Margaret teaches children and young adults with learning difficulties, and she runs evening classes and weekend and day classes to teach rag rug making, which she also teaches as part of the school examination curriculum on textiles.

In the past few years she has held several one-woman exhibitions, as well as exhibiting with other artists. In 1994, for example, she set up an exhibition of 100 pieces of work at Northleach Countryside Collection near Cirencester, Gloucestershire, and an exhibition of 90 of her pieces was held at Gloucester Folk Museum. During this exhibition, the people who visited it made a rug for the Museum.

Margaret has found that T-shirts are an excellent source of strips for rag rugs. They cut well, instantly becoming cord-like, and are easy to work with. She also uses a lot of spoiled, felted jumpers, which do not tend to unravel when they are cut into strips.

Although Margaret finds that corduroy and velvet are among the most difficult fabrics to use, some of her most stunning pieces are those that she has made from these very fabrics. Her pieces based on Turkish designs show how vivid and luxurious this kind of work can be. Other articles include a document case and a mixed media rug, which combines hooking and braiding techniques with a wide variety of materials, from chiffon and curtains to wool and corduroy.

This elegant document case is made from a folded oblong of hooked velvets. Velvet is a difficult fabric to hook, and when a smooth finish is needed, wide strips have to be used and the edges must be turned in as each hook is made. The inside of the case is lined in tartan fabric and edges are blanket stitched. The case is fastened with a simple button and loop.

Above: This hooked wall-hanging was inspired by Indian peacocks, and it has been worked in chiffon scarves and lining fabrics. When Margaret Docherty has finished it, the wall-hanging will include pieces of metallic fabrics of the kind often found in Indian textiles.

Right: The inspiration for this small hooked rug, worked in blue, white and yellow, was a Celtic tile. The design was enlarged and repeated, just as one might lay a pattern of ceramic tiles. Because the motif is repeated, the rug could be enlarged as wished.

Below: The Community Rug was made during an exhibition organized by Margaret Docherty for Gloucester Folk Museum. Members of the public were encouraged to "have a go", and this work is the result of a very successful experiment.

NANCY EDELL

Although she was born in Nebraska, Nancy Edell now lives and works in Canada. She trained as a film maker and animator in the United States and Britain in the late 1960s and was commended throughout Europe and the US for many of her films. However, she gradually came to realize that her real interest lay not in motion story telling but in template figures and their implied movements. She took up painting and drawing, and began to hook rugs and paint to create sets of work incorporating different media.

Her new interest in rag rugs was crystallized when she moved to Nova Scotia in 1980. There she was exposed to the local folk art traditions of rug hooking and to heavily figurative works. She hooks rugs and then works on huge oil paintings in a similar style that are part of a series of pictures. In this context her hooked rugs have moved away from their origins as humble door mats and have become a means of entering a new art form.

For Nancy the decision to hook rugs was a political as well as an artistic one. Her weaving is associated with the labour that women have performed for generations. By using rug hooking as part of her fine art work, Nancy feels that the image that is hooked is integral to the material itself, while on a painted canvas the image obscures the woven fabric that supports it.

Top: Stage Bath by Nancy Edell has a surreal quality. This Canadian artist started her career as a film maker and artist before turning her talents to rug hooking.

Centre: Nancy Edell is committed to figurative art and in her work attempts to balance form with content, control and spontaneity, and reality and illusion. In *Planting* she has managed to fuse the imagery of folk art and its medium into fine art.

Bottom: Nancy Edell was commissioned to create *Operating* by the exhibition Survivors in Search of a Voice, which was about breast cancer. Note the background's rich texture.

SARAH FLATMAN

Sarah Flatman is a rag rug artist in the loosest sense – she weaves scraps of paper to create three-dimensional objects – and her inspiration is drawn, appropriately, as she lives in Devon, from cream teas.

By day, she works as a dental nurse, but in her free time she creates objets d'art and performs as a juggler. She has recently returned from Kuala Lumpur, where she was circus assistant and juggled with a group of performance artists.

When it comes to making rag rugs, Sarah begins with sketches, which are developed into a series of collage drawings. The subjects – tea sets, china, cakes and so on – are drawn from various angles, so that a three-dimensional figure can be worked into a pattern. She tends to use the same inks and paints in her actual work as she does in her original design sheets. With the paints, she colours sheets of acid-free tissue paper, which are used for the weft when she begins to weave. She uses the tissue paper as one would use yarn, mixing strips together to achieve certain colour effects and surprises. One of the reasons she likes to use paper is the infinite selection of colours she can achieve with her paints.

The tissue paper is woven flat on to a frame. The teapot, for example, would be worked in two halves. Sarah puts darts in the completed woven pieces, which, in a process not unlike dressmaking, are made in upper and lower sections that are stitched together to create the three-dimensional shape.

Sarah goes to great pains to make sure that she achieves the right effects. To make the cakes, for instance, she visits dozens of cake shops, and her researches include visits to as many tea shops as possible. She is the only artist she knows who has

This mouth-watering Black Forest gateau, complete with a cream and cherry topping, was made by weaving acid-free tissue paper on a loom. The woven construction was then dyed and carefully cut and assembled, just as if it were a sculpture.

Strawberry shortcake and Devon slice were made from paper, which was then dyed. Sarah Flatman goes to great lengths to find suitably inspirational material, and she often has to destroy subjects that are not quite perfect enough – by eating them.

A complete strawberry tea set – tea pot, jug, cups and sauces, and a sugar bowl – have been formed out of woven tissue paper.
They are lined with a contrasting colour and decorated with small strawberries, also made by Sarah Flatman.

to eat her inspiration, but she feels that this is an essential ingredient of the artistic process.

She also turns to cookery books for help. To make cream horns, she read, it was necessary to roll out a piece of pastry 66cm (26in) long, so she had to weave a strip of pre-baked, coloured tissue paper 66cm (26in) long. Stitch this together, and you have a paper cream horn – and no mess in the kitchen!

BEN HALL

After taking a degree in painting and print-making and studying for a diploma in archaeology, Ben Hall took a master's degree in textiles at Goldsmith's College, London. Speaking of his own work, he reveals: 'I am drawn by the simple, honest style and humble origins of the rag rug that for me symbolize an aspect of social and domestic history that is more oral than written or academic. It is an example of what Emmanuel Cooper describes as "people's art", which for me places it at an interesting and irresistible confluence of meanings. As objects they have both charm and pathos that seem to echo the many-stranded relationship of home and family, be it close knit or tense. In my work I am trying to unravel some of these meanings, not just in terms of "home and hearth" but also in reflecting upon the changes in family and society that I have experienced or see as personal to my own life and sense of identity.'

Making items with textiles has led Ben to reflect on related and contemporary issues such as gender and identity. These have been important concerns in his work, not only as part of the 'end product' but also as an element in the process of thinking about and preparing his work. He believes that such work leads us back to the artist as an individual. 'The artist must necessarily find personal expression and meaning in that which they create. I see my own work as a basic response to various stimuli, ranging from the mundane to the quintessential, not only as an activity in its own right – making a visual or functional object – but also as a means of imparting, communicating or even exorcizing something of my own sense of self.'

Ben's recent pieces have been concerned with the centrality of 'work' and masculine identity. In an era of redundancy and changes in the work place he has become increasingly interested in the way that the myth or ideal of the 'working man' runs counter to social and economic realities, especially in relation to the home and family.

Minimal and almost Japanese in concept, *Optical Illusion* is a densely packed rug made by the prodded method. The background was worked in pieces from very pale, washed-out denim jeans, while newer denim fabric was used for the foreground.

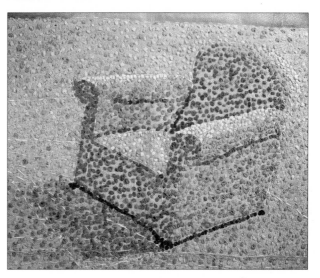

The front of Ben Hall's wall-hanging *Armchair*. It was worked by the prodding method, and the colours blend into each other in the manner of a pointillist painting. Like a pointillist painting, it is difficult to discern the image until you are a distance from it.

The reverse of Ben Hall's *Armchair*, which shows that it is possible to make a piece by this technique without packing the pieces in very densely. On the reverse, the chair is much clearer than it appears on the front due to the flat stitches.

Although it is also in the pointillist style, it is easier to make out the image in Ben Hall's *Flat Iron* because there is a sharper contrast between the tones used for the iron and its shadow and those used for the background.

NICKY HESSENBERG

Nicky Hessenberg has been interested in textiles and how to make and use them for as long as she can remember. After working in a machine knitting business for several years, she felt that she wanted to work with textiles in a way that was not limited by a machine and that freed her from commercial design constraints.

A course in constructed textiles, which she undertook as a mature student on a part-time basis, gave her an opportunity to develop other craft techniques that interest her, including small tapestry weavings, using a variety of fibres. It was a natural progression to rag rugs, which, requiring only basic tools and an easily mastered technique, allowed her to concentrate on colour, texture and shape without the limitations imposed by a loom.

Although she makes preliminary sketches, Nicky does not regard herself as a particularly skilful draughtswoman, and she tends to rely on her eye as she adds rags to – and removes them from – her rug designs. Making a rug can become a lengthy process because she often removes areas of colour if she is unhappy with her work in progress. This continual search for the right effect gives her work a spontaneity and immediacy and occasionally leads to some surprising results.

Ideas for designs come from all over the world, whether it is a simple walk along the beach or a striking architectural feature, and she uses photographs and pictures for reference. She is preparing to work on a series following on from 'The Christmas Turkey', which is based on Indian Mughal miniatures and uses birds and animals.

'The ideas come into my head all the time,' she says. 'The difficulty is getting them down on to a canvas fast enough, because I am not a fast worker. I am not a political person, although I have in the past completed a series of tapestry weavings ... to reflect my frustration at the destruction of the tropical rain forest, and maybe in the future I will develop these into rugs. At the moment I am concentrating on making rugs using simple geometric shapes and based on Amish patchwork quilts, trying to reproduce their vibrant use of colour. I love making rugs. I find it therapeutic, although sometimes frustrating, and I want to carry on enjoying myself.'

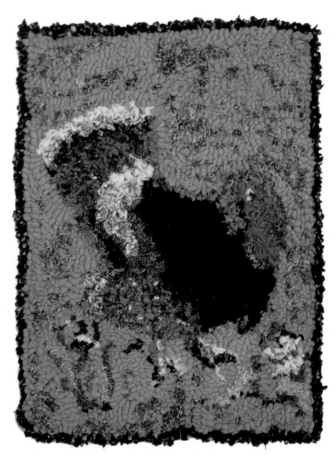

The Christmas Turkey, photographed by Ian Hessenberg, was based on Indian miniature paintings of birds and animals. Nicky Hessenberg begins with an idea and a pile of rags and just begins hooking. If she finds that an area of her work looks wrong, she simply removes the strips and re-works the section.

LIZ KITCHING

Liz Kitching was born in Cumbria, an area where rag rug making is something of a local tradition. She studied textile design before moving to London in the late 1970s, where she worked as a freelance textile designer with a number of architects and interior designers and for some private individuals. Her work led to her increasing interest in floor-coverings, and in 1983 she set up a workshop for the design and production of tufted rugs. It was not until 1988, however, that she produced her first collection of hand-painted floor cloths on canvas.

In 1989 she moved back to Cumbria, but she continued to work on tufted rugs and floor cloths, completing work that had been commissioned by the BBC and also working on new designs. After a year or two she began to feel that her work was outdated. She experimented with different techniques, ideas and materials to find a medium that would complement and harmonize with her new lifestyle and environment. The medium she found was rag rugs.

While she had been house hunting in Cumbria, she had noticed some very old rag rugs, often left behind in empty houses together with the odds and ends for which the departing owners had no further use. Liz always felt that they were very much a part of the house, even though they were dirty and threadbare.

Rag rug making is, of course, a regional tradition in the northeast of England, born out of necessity

Top right: Liz Kitching's *Cottage Garden No.1* is the first in a series of rugs with motifs drawn from cottage gardens. The stylized shapes, not unlike those seen in the late 1950s, have similarities to the motifs used in traditional rugs.

Bottom right: Cottage Garden No.3 is another in the series of rugs inspired by Liz Kitchings's Cumbrian country garden. Unlike much of her work, this is made entirely of cotton remnants.

This wonderful rug, *Proud Hen*, was made from a mixture of bright designer fabrics, including off-cuts from fabrics for Jaeger, Arabella Pollen and Jean Muir, mixed with remnants of classic tweeds. The tweeds give a wonderfully earthy hue for the speckled feathers, which gleam against the electric blue background.

and thriftiness, and many people still remember their older relatives making rugs. At about this time, Liz was given an old hook, made by her partner's great-grandfather who had been a blacksmith.

As soon as she began to hook her first rug, Liz felt a great sense of freedom, especially in the use of colour. In the previous media in which she had worked, the yarns had been sterile – a blue yarn would be just blue. When she began to use rags she found there was always an element of surprise and serendipity in the use of patterned fabrics and tweeds. The colours of a strip of rag look so different once they have been hooked.

Another great advantage of rag rug hooking from Liz's point of view is that there was no need to buy any machinery – all she needed was a frame and a hook. Nor need she always work in a studio – on fine days she can work in the garden, while on cold winter's days her work can be taken close to the fire. Considering that the finished rug is comparatively bulky, it is a mobile occupation.

Liz finds inspiration in the environment around her, especially the garden, in which there is the seasonal struggle to control nature as plants, paths and ornaments are rearranged and seeds are planted and crops reaped, while at the same time there is a perpetual desire to live in a wilderness. When she was working as a textile designer, her initial design process involved using a collage of painted paper, overdrawn loosely with a simple motif. Now that she is working with rags, she tends to use scraps of fabric instead of paper, with the design 'drawn' on the fabrics in simple embroidery stitches. This method allows Liz to see very quickly how the number of shapes and colours form the balance that she looks for in her compositions.

She uses a simple, home-made wooden frame and the old hook that she was given. She never dyes fabrics, which she feels unnecessary because she likes to build composite colours by using whatever is available. This, she feels, is the best way to make the finished composition successful and satisfying without being contrived.

Liz only occasionally exhibits her work, but she is happy to show her work privately to anyone who is fortunate enough to seek her out.

SUSAN LINDSAY

This Canadian rag rug artist works on a miniature scale. Her work is a collection of exquisite statements, often to do with the world of the home maker.

She remembers that when she was a child she had seen the older women of her neighbourhood hooking and braiding rugs. 'I was fascinated. For years I admired the worn and faded mats. In 1989 I began hooking. My pieces at first were small: I housed them, boxed them and framed them, and I eventually got up the courage to work on a rug. At present I am creating small pieces in silk and larger pieces in wool. My designs are often based on children's clothing.'

Her work 'The Clothes Line' was inspired by her memories of washing days when she was a child. 'Mom and I would work as a team, lifting, folding and pegging the wash. When sensing storms, we rushed outside to rescue our day's work. White and fresh, it spoke of a family story.'

Children's clothes have proved a fruitful source of inspiration for her: 'Children's clothes touch my heart. They are small, fragile and speak of innocence. They give me a sense of softness and warmth. There is a quiet loneliness and yet a strength in their tiny forms.'

Above right: Susan Lindsay works on a small scale, using wool, and on an even smaller scale with silks. *Hillary's Dress*, which measures 71 x 114cm (28 x 45in), was inspired by childhood memories and a love of faded old mats.

Right: This small, intricately made piece by Susan Lindsay is worked using the hooked method. *Old Blue Sweater*, which measures 67.5 x 72.5cm (27 x 29in), depicts the mis-shapen form of an old sweater, and the old fashioned colours used for the background frame add authenticity.

LU MASON

One of the main reasons Lu Mason began to make rag rugs was that she lived in a house with wooden floors but no carpets. She had no formal art school training but had always enjoyed working with fabrics, experimenting with silk and lino printing before turning to rag rugs.

Her American great-uncle had made rag rugs for his family and friends. Many of these were figurative, featuring the person for whom the rug was made and including the name of the person and the year it was made. Lu has drawn much inspiration from these rugs. Other influences on the designs and patterns on which she works are many and varied. She scours jumble sales, which not only gives her opportunities to find fabrics for the rugs but also to find the 1950s printed fabrics and 1920s ceramics that inspire her designs. She also admires Coptic tapestries, Ethiopian church paintings, African printed textiles and kelims, and these influences are clearly visible in her work.

Her preliminary design work consists of 'lots and lots of drawings', which she does until she has got a feel for the subject. She keep the stages of the design in her many sketch books. Lu makes both clipped and hooked rugs, and she has recently had a tufting gun specially adapted to take strips of cloth.

Lu used to teach regularly at local community centres, and from these she organized the making of a community rug. She also worked on many private commissions, making contacts initially through craft fairs and later by word of mouth recommendation. However, she did not enjoy working to commission and was reluctant to continue rag rug making as a business. She therefore decided to train as an occupational therapist and now works as one on a full-time basis.

Above: This hand hooked rug, *Woman Standing in the Wind,* is full of movement. It drew its inspiration from several sources, including Coptic textiles and kelim rugs.

Below: The Sailor would not be out of place in an exhibition of Russian Constructivist paintings. The shape of the clothes and the pose of the people contribute to the strong design.

ALISON MORTON

After studying at Dartington College of Art, Devon, and taking a degree course at Manchester College of Art, Alison Morton worked in industry for six years. She spent a year working in a knitwear factory in Lancashire, before designing woven textiles in a woollen mill in Wales. In 1976 she set up on her own. Her first rag rug was woven as an experiment for her own use. This was so successful that she started to weave rugs commercially, and she became interested in all types of rag rugs, even beginning a collection of tools for hooking and prodding. The local guild of weavers and spinners asked her to take a one-day course on hooking and prodding, and this was the first of many classes that she has since taken, mostly in her own workshop.

Her techniques have changed only slightly over the years – plain weave leading on to twill and tufted rugs – but she has added knitted rags to give a sculptural effect to the wall-hangings. The main development has been the ways in which she combines various techniques to create different textures.

Alison works out her ideas directly on the loom or by selecting the colours with which she is going to work. She does not make any initial sketches. Colour is, perhaps, the main emphasis of her rugs, which she creates almost as if they were Impressionist sculptures.

Her rags come from jumble sales and charity (thrift) shops or are given to her by friends. Because she does not dye the fabrics, she needs to collect considerable amounts to give her the range of colours she needs. She uses both synthetic and natural fabrics, although for the woven rugs she prefers to use mainly knitted and soft woven fabrics, which beat down well and cover the warp. She keeps the thinner cottons for her hooked rugs.

She sells her woven rugs from her workshop and from exhibitions. She also makes hooked and prodded rugs purely for her own enjoyment and as demonstration pieces for workshops.

Alison Morton finds that one of the most satisfying aspects of weaving is the subtle range of colours that she can achieve. The two woven rag rugs shown here were made with plain weave.

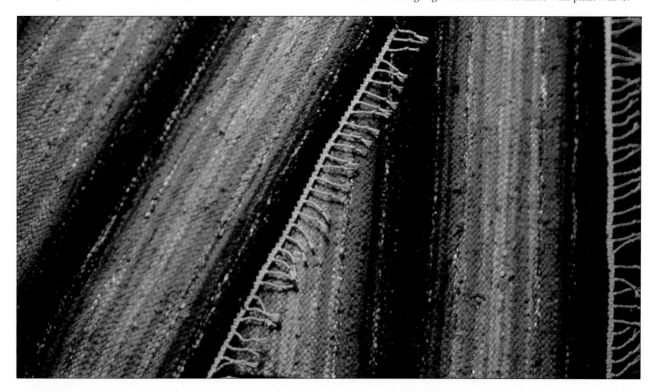

LIZZIE REAKES

This young British rag rug maker has a very distinctive style. She makes her multi-coloured, unusually shaped rugs, wall-hangings, mirror frames and so on by hooking, and often shears the pile when the work is finished.

Lizzie Reakes comes from London, and after leaving school she studied textiles before beginning a course on carpet design. She has always been interested in surface pattern, rather than fashion, and the carpet design course included three industrial placements, which gave her valuable experience of all aspects of textile design. The first placement was with a group of industrial designers who specialized in low-budget office designs; the second was with Janet Beran, who designed woven textiles, mostly for the Australian and American markets; the third was with a company specializing in domestic and contract carpeting.

Towards the end of her course, Lizzie realized that she was more interested in the craft aspects of design rather than its industrial applications, and she chose rag rug hooking because she enjoyed both the physical activity involved in wielding the hook and the freedom that the technique offers. In addition, unlike craft processes such as machine embroidery, there are few rag rug makers working commercially, which makes it easier for her to make a living.

Starburst is another in Lizzie Reakes's series of rugs based on astronomical themes. This rug was worked by the hooking method in the traditional semicircular, hearth rug shape.

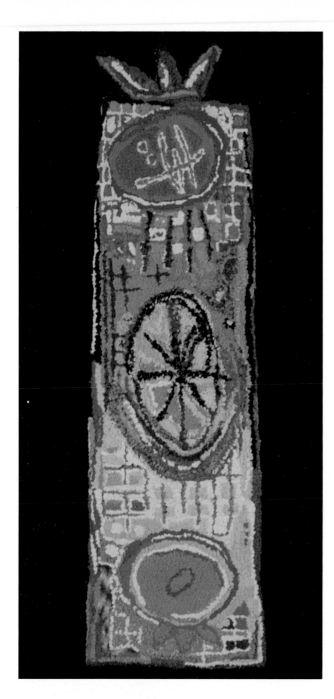

Above: Both these chair pads were made by hooking, although different kinds of fabrics were used on each. The design was worked out on the hessian before the hooking was completed, and the finished pieces were cropped to give a tight pile that resembles velvet.

Left: Battenberg is one of a series of wall-hangings inspired by the colour blue and by the textile industry and graphic style of the 1950s. Rather than being simply symmetrical, the top has been decorated with an interesting three-feathered shape.

In the last year of her course Lizzie joined the Rag Rug Society of the UK, and this helped her to make several important contacts. While she was demonstrating rag rug making at craft fairs, she began to realize that many of the other crafts being offered were far quicker to work, and consequently less expensive, than rag rugs. She therefore decided to concentrate on smaller projects that she could complete quickly, and she came up with the unusual idea of creating pieces of jewellery. Through her contacts

in the Rag Rug Society she began to exhibit her work together with that of other rug makers, and she is now a regular contributor to themed exhibitions.

As her work has become better known, Lizzie has received many commissions. The Chelsea Craft Fair, held in London in 1993, brought her to the attention of a wide range of people, and she has worked on commissions for clients in North America. So far, the largest piece she has made is 2 x 2m (6ft 6in x 6ft 6in), but the frame she generally uses is 1.3m (50in) wide, which limits the width of her work, although it can be as long as she wishes.

Eureka, the 'hands-on' children's museum in Halifax, Yorkshire, has acquired one of Lizzie's rugs, which it displays in its recycling section, and another of her works can be seen at her old college at Kidderminster.

Today Lizzie teaches from time to time. She enjoys working with all age groups and says that she is often surprised and excited by the unusual pieces that are produced by conventional-looking people. She has acted as artist in residence at a number of schools, when she has worked with visually impaired people. She also lectures on her own work and on the traditions of rag rug making, and she emphasizes the importance both of recycling old fabrics and of using modern materials.

Lizzie finds inspiration in contemporary rather than traditional designs. Many of her early pieces were based on the tarot and on space and the stars, but she also draws on the things she sees around her, including everyday life in a city, fast food and football. Her rugs reflect her enthusiasms – if she likes a subject it will sooner or later find its way into a piece of work. She has, for example, produced a series of rugs on a blue theme, inspired by Joni Mitchell's album Blue. She has also been influenced by the pop art and abstract expressionism that were popular in the 1960s.

Lizzie keeps a scrap book in which she records her designs, which are usually on a fairly small scale. These are later translated into rugs and hangings by the simple expedient of attaching a marker to the end of a stick and transferring the designs on to the hessian in large, loose lines.

She finds it easy to use up to 100 colours in a rug but is now trying to be more minimal. Unlike many rag rug makers, Lizzie prefers to work with synthetic materials. She has used rubber washing-up gloves, which she found difficult to hook, crisp packets, which work very well in jewellery, where the paper

Lizzie Reakes developed *Outer Spacers* from astronomical themes, but decided to give the stars a starfish-like quality. The rug has been worked in deep, warm colours, and it has been fitted with hangers so that it can suspended from a wooden baton.
(Rug lent by Camilla Giles.)

glints and glistens, and acrylics, especially those mixed with metallic threads, which tend to be colour fast and are easy to work with. Other favourite materials are nylon sheets in garish colours and old stretch-covers for three-piece suites.

She has recently been working for the UK Crafts Council's exhibition on recycling and has contributed to several books.

ALI RHIND

Ali Rhind is a textile artist who has produced many publicly commissioned pieces. She uses two traditional techniques – hooking and prodding – to create colourful rugs and hangings with contemporary designs, while at the same time drawing on the rich social history of the northeast of England and the place in which she works, Woodham Colliery Museum.

Ali trained as a sculptor and in the 1970s she became part of the Artist in the Community movement, which encourages artists to work with local communities, bringing together people of different ages and backgrounds to create joint projects. She found that working together in this way encouraged people to discover new skills, adapt old ones and often take a fresh look at art and creative activities in general.

The women in the community art project were originally rather intimidated by the sort of 'art' Ali practised, so she decided to take a different tack and trained in the indigenous craft activity of the northeast – 'proggy' and 'hooky' mat making. In this way she was able to prove to the women in the project that the rug making techniques that they and their ancestors had been practising for years was, in fact, an art form in its own right.

Ali learned rug making techniques from an elderly woman called Peggy Webber. She felt that it was better to work with the local community in a partnership, rather than showing them, as an outsider, what to do and make. So, while she taught them new skills, they taught her by drawing on their history and traditions.

Below: The Magic Carpet, a wall-hanging commissioned by Sunderland City Art Gallery, depicts characters from classic children's stories, including animals. It hangs up in the library, but is taken down so that children can sit on it for story-telling sessions.

Above: This cushion cover, *Carmen Miranda*, has been made by the hooked method and is a good example of the artist's wry sense of humour.

Right: Instead of the usual Christmas baubles, *The Christmas Tree* has a garland strung from top to bottom that looks like a streak of lightning. The zigzag flash makes it look as if the tree is being rooted in the earth.

Rag rugs have been a tradition in this part of Britain for many years. Competitions were held in working men's clubs, women's institutes and at the annual leek (vegetable) shows. All the mining communities in Newcastle and the surrounding areas took part in mat making. One tradition was that of the mat club, where a group of people would each pay a small amount of money every week to a mat maker and, when their name came to the top of the list, they would have the finished rug. Another tradition in the northeast is that when a mat was

finished, the youngest child in the family had to roll on it to bring good luck. Whenever possible, a new rug would be made for Christmas Day.

Rug making in this area was widely associated with poverty – rugs were often made to provide additional warmth on beds – and as people became wealthier they often stopped wanting to make them.

The tools used in rag rug making are a fascinating part of the history. In South Shields, for example, the 'fids', the tools used by fishermen to mend their nets, were also used for prodding. In Cumbria, a farming area, rams' horns were used as prodders. In Wallsend, fine turned tools were made by apprentices in the shipyards, and in mining communities crude metal hooks and 'proggers' were made in blacksmiths' shops in the pit yards.

When she had learned the basics of rag rug making, Ali invited local people to join a mat making group. The response was excellent, and for six years 25 people met twice a week to make rugs. As people left the group, they set up new groups. The venture gathered people together, and they learned from each other, reviving the old, traditional skills and passing them on to new generations. Ali encouraged them to experiment with new colours and materials, and she found that: 'People are often happier to work a picture on a rug than on a canvas. By being able to create their own designs and patterns on the rugs, the work belonged to them.'

Sometimes people worked on group projects; at other times they worked individually. In 1976 the group held an exhibition of their work in the library in North Shields. Much of the work was humorous, and most of the materials used were man-made fabrics such as acrylic, jersey and crimplene, which do not wear well and are best used for wall-hangings rather than floor-coverings.

In 1988 Ali Rhind and Jenny Lorian organized a group project of 24 hooked panels called 'A Day in the Life'. Each panel represented one hour in the day of the maker's life. The scenes are largely domestic, some are funny, others are touching. The piece toured in an exhibition called Hooky Matters.

Another of Ali's many public commissions is 'The Flying Carpet', which she created for a library. It depicts universal characters from children's stories. The rug hangs on a wall, unless there is a story-telling session, when it is taken down for the children to sit on.

Below: The design of *Dog Lying on a Rug* was inspired partly by Ali Rhind's love of dogs and partly by the motifs found on medieval tapestries, which often include dogs surrounded by flowers. Here, Ali was attempting to produce a twentieth-century interpretation of the medieval theme.

In 1992 Ali was chosen from a number of textile artists who had been asked to submit schemes for Wansbeck General Hospital in Ashington, a low-energy hospital designed by Powell Moya to serve the east coast of Northumberland. The design consisted of four separate panels, each 365 x 91cm (12 x 3ft). 'Sun', 'Wind' and 'Sea' would hang horizontally on one wall, with 'Earth' hanging vertically to the right on an adjacent wall.

The idea behind the hangings was that the sun, sea and wind are all energy sources, and, because the hospital runs on low energy, there was an obvious link. Satellite photographs of hurricanes were adapted and used. Because the hospital serves a wide location, covering an area ranging from the sea to mining communities, the elements appealed to the different communities. The colours had to fit in with the colour scheme of the hospital, and because it was a public building, the hangings had to be fire-proofed.

More than 100 people within the community worked on the wall-hangings at three different sites, and the local people who use the hospital have the satisfaction of knowing that they worked on the project. The hangings are mainly out of the reach of hands, except for 'Earth', which has a coal face on its lower quarter, but it is worked in dark colours so that it is not harmed by being touched.

When Ali works, the design is always the starting point, although she often collects bits and pieces to build up ideas for her designs. 'Proddy' or 'proggy' rugs are worked from the back, and in order to get

Ali Rhind was invited by architects Powell Moya to create a wall-hanging for Wansbeck General Hospital, and the wall-hanging was to reflect the fact that the hospital was run on low-energy principles. It was made in four sections, each of which was based on one of the natural elements.

an even texture all over the rug, she has to cut fabrics of different weights to different widths – the heavier the fabric, the narrower the strip; the lighter the fabric, the wider the strip. Ali uses 10oz hessian, which she finds ideal for her method of prodding (see page 30); this is more difficult to do with burlap, which is a finer fabric.

Below: A section of the community project *A Day in the Life*. Different rug makers were asked to contribute by making a panel to depict a different hour in a woman's day. Some of the pieces were humorous, others thought-provoking.

DEBBIE SINISKA

Debbie Siniska's first interest in crafts was with beads, especially loomwork. An exhibition of Turkish weaving stimulated her curiosity about the possibilities inherent in fabric weaving, and she began to experiment with colour and texture. The limitations imposed by the loom – there is little scope for change and innovation during the weaving process – led her to search for a craft that would give her flexibility of method and fluidity of design, yet allow her to make beautiful and functional articles.

It was during a visit to Jenni Stuart-Anderson (see pages 106–108) that she was introduced to rag rug making, and Jenni lent her a shuttle hook – at last she had found the medium and technique with which she could work. Such was Debbie's enthusiasm that she cut up everything she could with which to practise the new craft, including not only her scarves but even her own clothes.

Her first rug included a sun motif, and she now uses a moon face in a sun as her logo. Many of her designs are inspired by the sun and moon. As a realist, Debbie prefers to use images that she can translate directly into her chosen medium. She likes to make simple, bold statements, and many of her rugs are based on the colours that she has immediately to hand. The colour of an individual garment will often spark off an idea for a design, and she sometimes begins with that colour, allowing the design to evolve as she works.

Ideas for designs may come from something as small as a postage stamp if there is movement and life in the image. When she has an idea for a rug she often lays out the garments from which she will cut the rag strips on the floor, moving the colours around until she is satisfied with the arrangement. Her whole

Comet Sun was one of the first designs that Debbie Siniska ever created, and the designs of many of her subsequent pieces have been influenced by the sun, stars and moon. This particular image – a moon face in the sun – has now been turned into a wood block and is used as part of her logo.

This small mat, *For Sarah, Bird of Paradise*, is based on a theme that recurs in Debbie Siniska's work. Note how the hooking of the background emphasizes the movement of the bird.

family sometimes becomes involved in the process. She feels that the simple patterns that develop in this way work well in the finished rug, and she rarely goes through the process of transferring the outline to a grid and then drawing it on the hessian, preferring to work freehand.

She prefers to work with knitted garments, which have a natural 'spring' and which keep their shape. She also uses old T-shirts and sweatshirts and other

Above: This small mat, with its design of shells, was made only with recycled materials, including the peanut sack that was used for the backing and that dictated the size of the finished rug. The swirling background, which suggests the sea, and the pink shell in the foreground make this an ideal rug for a porch of a seaside cottage.

Below: Flying Crows is a small wall-hanging made with a shuttle hook. The backing fabric was a peanut sack. The black crows are shown as silhouettes as they fly across the cloudy sky.
(Rug lent by Michael Ball.)

fabrics that are closely knitted and do not fray. She finds crimplene a hard, unsympathetic fabric, but likes using flannel trousers and scarves. She is an avid attender of jumble sales and also uses garments given to her by her friends. She does not dye her fabrics, finding sufficient variety of colour in the garments themselves.

Debbie uses a speed shuttle because it is quick and flexible. She finds that she can easily make curves in her designs with the shuttle, and, because the rug is worked from the back, she feels that it takes on a different dimension. She also enjoys the ceremony of turning the completed rug around. Debbie does not clip the loops of her rugs, leaving them to create a rather cabbage-like effect. She usually backs her rugs, which provides an anchor for the loops, and she sometime includes a layer of pot pourri or lavender between the rug and the backing.

Many of her works have been sold, and Debbie also undertakes commissions, including designs worked to commemorate loved pets, to illustrate dreams or simply to celebrate a favourite colour. She has recently received a commission from a Canadian client to create a large rug in various shades of yellow.

In addition to making and selling rugs, which she does partly in association with a group of other artists working in different media, Debbie teaches and organizes courses on rug making, which she also demonstrates at exhibitions. Through her contacts with the Rag Rug Society of the UK, Debbie was commissioned by the Fan Museum, Greenwich, London, for which she designed a fan-shaped rug with a pattern of Chinese dragons. She also makes small items because she wants the articles she makes to be within reach of most pockets, not just those of wealthy clients, and she has embarked on a series of pictures, small-scale rugs, chair seats and friezes. She has also made a highly unusual semicircular rug that is designed to go above a door frame (see pages 131–132).

LYNNE STEIN

Lynne Stein's fascination with design was originally stimulated by Italian designs of the late 1960s and by the psychedelia of the period. She has long been interested in exploring the potential of a variety of media, and this encouraged her interest in rag rug making.

There is no tradition of rag rug making in her family, although it was associated with the textile industry. Her grandmother was in the trimmings business, and Lynne, who inherited her boxes of buttons and beads, remembers that her grandmother 'did not let me pass through my teens without crocheting a collar for almost every dress I possessed'.

Before she began to make rugs, Lynne trained as an art therapist, and she worked with people with many different needs and problems and of every possible age and background. Although her work was rewarding, she felt frustrated that her creativity was not being used to the full.

Like many rag rug makers, she is mainly self-taught. She had attended many courses, learning to weave, dye, spin and make paper and felt, before going to a weekend workshop run by Ali Rhind (see pages 97–100), where she saw rag rugs made by both the hooked and prodded methods. This short course awakened her to the excitement of working with the enormous range of colours, textures and patterns that are possible with rag rugs. She was also intrigued by the recycling that is involved in the process as well as by the possibilities for moving the craft beyond its original intentions and associations.

She says: 'It is a medium that is very immediate and direct. [It] lends itself extremely well to the translation of graphic imagery. Its resultant qualities can be extremely painterly, and to some extent sculptural. I consider myself, in fact, to be more of a

"painter", who happens to use fibre and fabric, than a needlewoman.'

Lynne has a genuine love of, and respect for, some of the historic and traditional rag rugs, especially some of the very finely hooked rugs from the United States, which she found especially inspiring when she was beginning to experiment with the craft. However, advances in technology – synthetic dyes, man-made fibres and fabrics and innovative tools such as tufting guns – have all contributed to her exploration of new ways of working.

Her work with community groups in different parts of Britain has brought her into contact with people who can still recount community and family traditions of rag rug making, and she has been given – and gratefully received – many old tools that people had kept as relics of their family history. She says that often, when she gives demonstrations, she

This piece, *Persian Tile*, was created from mixed fibres and fabrics by the gun-tufting method. The design was developed from Lynne Stein's own collection of artefacts and decorative items.

Above left: Two Camels is a gun-tufted piece that was worked with a mixture of fabrics. It forms part of a series based on mythological beasts, and its inspiration comes from cave drawings and children's paintings. The artist enjoys creating small pieces with irregular sides and edges.

Above right: Lynne Stein's *Rosie at Midnight* was made by the gun-tufting method with a variety of fabrics and fibres. The artist was inspired by children's drawings, especially those of her son, and the work was created especially for an exhibition held in Los Angeles.

frequently hears people say: 'Oh, I remember my mother doing that with us.' Most of the people with whom she comes in contact are more familiar with clipped and prodded rugs than hooked ones, and she finds that they are often surprised by the compactness that can be achieved by hand hooking.

Her first public commission was for the borough council of Trafford, Manchester, which wanted a wall-hanging for Timperley Library. Her brief was to teach and involve various community groups in the making of a rag rug. It was during this period that she discovered the positive and beneficial effects of rag rug making, and as she worked she became increasingly aware of the craft's beneficial effects, both social and creative, on the community with whom she was working.

Since then she has undertaken several commissions that have involved carrying out research, both geographical and historical, in an area. Some of her large-scale projects are detailed, didactic works, which stretch to the limit the potential of the craft. These pieces include unusual materials, such as human hair and plastic bags, which she uses more for their effect

than for any striving towards authenticity.

Much of her work in recent years has been commissioned by local authorities throughout Britain for libraries, hospices, health centres and other civic buildings, including art centres. She also exhibits about four times each year and undertakes private commissions. In addition, she runs rag rug workshops within the national adult education system and in secondary schools.

In her work, Lynne uses surface colour and form, especially the juxtaposition and combination of a range of materials, to explore her themes. Her influences range from mythological beasts and folklore to the patterns and colours found in contemporary interior design. She may sketch a design on the back of an empty cereal packet or she may make some more detailed drawings, including colour and collage studies, in her sketch book. The discovery of a particular fabric or yarn can dictate the colour and content of a piece of work.

When she begins work, she always drafts the design on the hessian backing with an indelible marker. If it is to be a small piece, she will use a frame measuring 60 x 60cm (2 x 2ft). Larger pieces are worked on an adjustable rug frame, which is almost 1.8m (6ft) wide. Although she will have planned the basic colour scheme and composition before she begins, Lynne always works intuitively, and the design is often worked out as it is hooked.

Lynne uses a vast array of fabrics and, because her work is made to be displayed as wall-hangings, she is little concerned about fraying and colour fastness. Her work is finely hooked and extremely dense, and she can, therefore, use almost any fabric she wishes, including the net bags in which satsumas are sold in supermarkets. Because colour and textural contrasts are so important to her, she often places smooth, shiny silks next to coarse, fraying furnishing linen, and fluorescent T-shirt material next to bouclé yarn. She find fabrics such as patterned crimplene, felted wool, T-shirts and sweatshirts particularly easy to work with.

Her palette is usually bright and colourful. Fuchsia pink will be placed next to scarlet, and she often introduces silvers and golds into her work. Because dyeing can be such a time-consuming process, she uses very little dye, relying instead on the vast range of colours she finds in jumble sales and in the old garments and fabrics that are passed on to her from friends and students.

She often uses naturally or synthetically dyed fleece, which she hooks very tightly to create a dense pile, which she then carves and sculpts with sharp scissors to create new effects.

Because her work is so detailed and complex, Lynne uses a hook rather than a prodder, a tool she feels is better suited to simpler, more geometric designs. She also uses an electric tufting gun, which has allowed her to create parts of rugs in relief, which she does by cramming the backing fabric with rags. The tufting gun also allows her to incorporate strings of beads and sequins into her designs. If she tried to hook these by hand they would break.

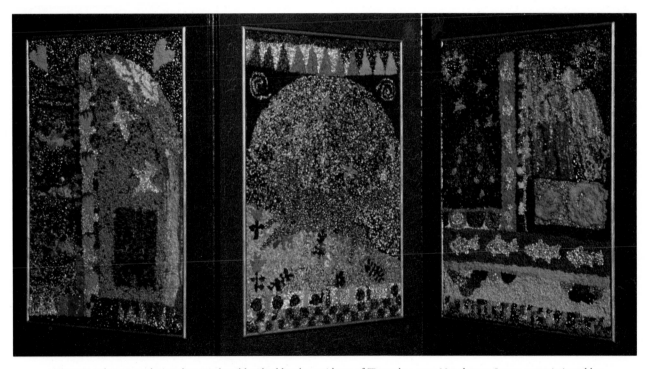

Screen is a three-part design that was hand-hooked by the residents of Timperley, near Manchester. It was commissioned by Trafford Borough Council in association with the North Western Arts Board and the Community Arts Workshop. It is now housed in the Coppice Avenue Library, Trafford, Manchester.

JENNI STUART-ANDERSON

Jenni Stuart-Anderson trained as an architectural designer, and she lives in an isolated cottage that she built herself around the ruins of an old cottage. Although born in Wales, she lived and worked in London before moving to the country.

The birth of her daughter and the isolation of early motherhood led her to look for a creative outlet that would not be expensive and that could be picked up and put down easily, and she asked a local woman, Doris Tunley, to teach her how to make rugs. Doris, the daughter of a local blacksmith, had been involved in rug making all her life and had made rugs herself for over 50 years. As a child she had cut fabric into pieces for her mother, and when, as an adult she made her own rugs, her husband cut the pieces for her. She had used a speed shuttle since she was 14 years old and taught Jenni how to use it.

Jenni finds the link between finding the old materials that she used to build her cottage and finding old fabrics to create works of art a strong one. She also enjoys being able to combine her interests – she sometimes uses her rag rugs as yoga mats, and she has made five-pointed star mats for herself and her daughter to sit on when they attend festivals.

Jenni started by making small mats with simple pictorial and textural effects. As her skills and techniques developed, her works became larger and more complex. Her inspiration comes from natural sources – leaves and shells, for example – and her other interests – astrology, New Age healing processes and Native American culture, particularly Senecca, the wolf clan. 'The Red Indian culture is an ecologically sound lifestyle,' she says, 'with respect for other life forms. The planet, "mother", is treated with respect. Chief Seattle wrote in the 1800s about how we will choke in our own filth if we carry on living as we are.' She admires the Native Americans for taking only what they needed from nature.

Flying Eagle was designed to be an easily transportable rug that Jenni Stuart-Anderson could take with her to festivals and other outdoor events. It reveals two of the major influences on her work – mosaics and Native American culture.

This rug, with its image of a huge rose, is worked in shades of pink, from a delicate pale pink through to bright fuchsia.

Several of Jenni's rugs are based on mazes, which she finds powerful symbols, and labyrinths, which are often womb-like in appearance. She also searches through library books for ideas on which to base her designs and collects postcards. Her daughter's early drawings have also been enlarged and translated into rugs.

She has made rugs for clients that interpret their dreams. After long discussions with them, she comes up with designs to visualize the dreams. One client, for example, had dreamed of power associated with an animal, and Jenni made a rug that included a bear. Another had a dream about healing and something – hands or a root – growing, and Jenni eventually designed a rug that looked like a lotus, with flames floating on water. One of her best known rugs is an astrological one, with a sun face at the centre and the signs of the zodiac around the edge.

Jenni works to commission, but she also holds workshops in the West Midlands, London and Dorset, teaching about 200 people each year. She finds that her classes are mainly attended by women, although she is happy to teach men. She feels that rag rug making is 'an unsung women's art, with a small a. Everyone can do it.' She says that many women find that they cannot draw and that painting and drawing are not creative experiences for them, but when they begin to work with rag rugs they build up their confidence. She adds that one of the comments she hears most often from women who are attending one of her day or weekend courses is: 'A whole day to myself!' Clients tend to find her by word of mouth, although people who have attended her courses sometimes return to buy her work. Because it is difficult to charge for making rugs, she has worked out her own system and charges by the square foot.

In common with many teachers of rug making, she finds that most students are scared, or do not know how, to begin drawing. She encourages them to concentrate on colour and texture for their first attempts at prodding, which are done on hessian

Above: The design of *Rhiannon* was taken from a drawing that Jenni Stuart-Anderson's daughter made when she was three years old. The rug captures both the naïvety and joy that is found so much in children's drawing.

Below: This circular rug is based on the themes occurring in the Celtic zodiac. It reflects Jenni Stuart-Anderson's interest in mazes and labyrinths, which she has always found to be relevant and powerful symbols.

held in their laps. Later, she suggests tracing or photo-copying images that they want to turn into rugs.

In the part of England where Jenni lives, prodders or 'proggers' were made from nails attached to a wooden handle. 'Bodgers', a tool with jaws like a spring clip, were also used, and chair makers use a larger version of this tool for caning chairs.

Jenni uses a speed shuttle for most of her rugs. She has modified it to meet her own requirements, and her version is now available (see page 34). In common with other rag rug makers, Jenni gets most of her materials from jumble sales and from friends and old students. She uses a Rigby strip cutter from Maine, which speeds up the laborious process of cutting strips. The cutter can be set to different widths – the speed shuttle takes strips just under 1cm (3/8 in) wide, compared with the 6mm (1/4 in) often used with a hand hook.

Jenni's rugs contain embellishments that would surprise a purist. One of her many eagle rugs has a spiral of fleece worked into it, while a braided rug is decorated with gold chain stitch. She often lets the fabrics she is using suggest changes in designs as she works. If, for example, she runs out of one colour she is quite happy to introduce another. As she says, it is important to be flexible when you are making a rag rug: 'The tradition was to use what was to hand. The rug you end up with may not be what you intended, but it may be better. Let the rug grow organically.' Interestingly, some early American rugs have a small patch of brown in a blue sky, and sometimes this is done today to make rugs look old.

When she is working on her own rugs Jenni tends to simplify shapes rather than rationalize them, as she did with 'Mel', a rug hooked in memory of her dog (see page 130).

◆

CARMEL TREANOR

After studying at a college of art and design, Carmel Treanor studied decorative surfaces in a degree course at Kidderminster College. Hand tufting and rag rugging were options on the course, and she chose them because she felt they gave the most freedom. 'This medium is so tactile, and I believe it to be the most exciting and expressive. I found the carpet yarns and materials available at college, carpet manufacturers and so on to be limiting, and my interest in translating my designs successfully led me to the Indian sari shops, which are abundant in Wolverhampton. This opened a whole new and exciting palette for me to work from, and I bought many remnants and pieces of cloth from these wonderful shops.'

Carmel's inspiration comes from jewellery and

This working detail is from a rag rug made by Carmel Treanor by the gun-tufting method. The strips of fabric have to be cut very fine if the technique is to work successfully.

Left: Carmel Treanor's *Banana Rug* measures 50 x 130cm (20 x 51in). This detail shows the vibrant colours of the fabrics that have been used and the way in which the sparkling thread has been combined with the silk, netting and cottons to create a glowing image set in a dark background.

Below: The science fiction work of the same name inspired Carmel Treanor's *Dune*. The central motif looks like a planet, surrounded by vapour rings as it flies off into space. The piece was worked with a tufting gun.

cloth patterns, especially those from the Far East and Africa. Some of her early work was translated more literally from her painting. Now, when she is designing, she begins by painting faces, alive with ritual face paints, together with the beaded costumes and head-dresses. From the drawing she starts to abstract isolated areas, and from these a design for a floor-covering emerges.

She works with a Hoffman tufting gun, with the backing firmly stretched on to an upright metal frame. She used to use equal proportions of yarn and fabric, employing the yarn mainly as the background colour and the rags for detail. More recently she has started to work in a more abstract style, preferring to let the designs evolve as she is working. She likes to introduce sparkling threads, silks, cottons and netting into the designs.

She sold her first work, 'Sparkler', to a private buyer who saw her work at the exhibition The Young Designers at the Business Design Centre. Through other exhibitions her work became known to a wider audience, and she has been approached

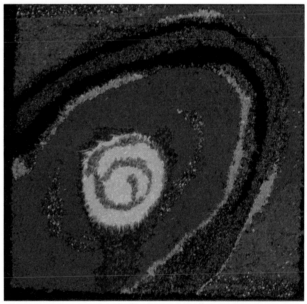

by a UK brewery to undertake a commission for a public house in Wolverhampton. She has also completed two images of tribal people for private commissions.

In addition to running workshops, she has done some teaching in schools and workshops.

AMANDA TOWNEND

After her initial studies in textile and carpet design, Amanda Townend set up her own workshop where she is still making mats and carpets. All her rugs and carpets are made with recycled materials and old-fashioned printed fabrics. Her grandmother and other relatives from the northeast of England had made rag rugs, and Amanda loves the process of discovering the history of the pieces of fabric she uses in her work.

She was involved in the Ragtime exhibition and contributed to the 'A Day in the Life' project, organized by Ali Rhind and Dee Gilder for the Shipley Art Gallery (see page 99). She exhibits her work throughout the north of England and has held workshops for a wide variety of students, including children, people with special needs and the elderly.

She has just completed a series of workshops at the People's History Museum, Manchester, which ran in tandem with an exhibition called The People's Art, which included folk art from Yorkshire and Humberside ranging from rag rugs to fairground art.

Above: Examples of brightly coloured, multi-textured mats made by the hooked and prodded methods.

Below: Here a hearts design has been made from different coloured sweaters cut into strips and hooked lying on a multi-coloured prodded background.

JUJU VAIL

Originally from Canada but now living in London, Juju Vail began by specializing in millinery, knitwear and textile design. She designed a range of hand-knitted sweaters with designs based on folk crafts, old quilts, cross stitch and rag rugs, but when plans to translate the woollen designs into cotton for the US market fell through, she moved to London to study textile design. The course she took was aimed at people who wanted to go into the textile industry and was not craft-based, as she had hoped. In order to succeed on the course, Juju needed to find an academic field, and she decided to study the traditions and roots of the indigenous craft techniques of Canada

Before about 1850, when hessian (burlap) began to be made, hooked rag rugs as we know them today could not be made. The only way they could have been worked would have been to have used linen as a backing fabric and to withdraw threads to create a sufficiently loose weave.

Juju Vail is seen working on a piece of hooked rug. Unlike most of the artists whose work is illustrated in this book, she prefers to work in her lap rather than on a frame. Before beginning work, she stitches a bias-cut strip along the edge of the design, and hooks right up to it.

Just a few of the wonderfully flamboyant hats that Juju Vail has made by the hand hooking method. The tops of the hats have been created by a combination of appliqué and machine embroidery. These hats are very warm and surprisingly light to wear.

This small sample piece from Juju Vail's portfolio shows a technique that has been revised and expanded by the artist. The edging was made by cutting a piece of fabric on the bias and filling it with a strip cut from a blanket. It is then stitched to the hessian backing before the work is hooked.

Above: In addition to the beaver, this hooked rug includes motifs based on birch bark and the traditional embroidery of the Eastern Woodland Native Americans.

Right: Juju Vail uses a sort of story-board technique to work out the tones and designs for her work. The beaver was chosen as a motif representing the conflicting ideas of hard work and the European colonization of Canada.

1 1 2

Juju's studies led her to look closely at her own Canadian roots. She remembers the family house, which contained quilts and rag rugs that had been in her family for generations, and she remembers as a child being surrounded by folk art. Her dissertation notes: 'As with the language, the folk arts of Canada are lumped together with those of the United States, even though folk arts, by definition, are an indigenous, domestic expression.' Her researches covered all aspects of Canadian folk art, but she decided to learn the skills of the rag rug maker and to discover all she could about the craft's history in Canada: 'They had an under-recognized history and development, which echoed that of Canada. Hooking skills were taken on board and practised.'

Juju's designs are drawn from a variety of sources. She keeps a sketch book, and paints, draws and makes collages. She sometimes develops her designs by scanning them into a computer and rearranging the images to create new patterns and shapes.

Because she regards the process as environmentally unfriendly, Juju does not dye her work. She uses only recycled materials, including plastic bags and tin foil, as well as feathers and glittery fabrics. She collects large quantities of material from charity (thrift) shops and jumble sales. She tries to collect a number of shades of each colour so that she can build up a palette from which to blend the motifs in her rugs. She works by hooking and sometimes cuts a pile in the finished rug.

Among the public commissions she has undertaken is a large rug for the Canadian High Commission, which was established in 1880 to encourage British emigration to Canada. The rug, which measures 1 x 1.4m (3ft 3in x 4ft 7in), hangs in the office of the Cultural Attaché. The design for the rug was inspired by the beaded souvenirs and Victorian-style pin-cushions made by Native Canadians in the late nineteenth century in order to promote the products and identity of the country and thereby encourage tourism and emigration. These

This detail of Juju Vail's *Souvenir of Hochelaga* shows how modern materials and rich colours have been used to create a rug that recalls the button boots that were sometimes made in bead-work or in fabric in the late nineteenth century and sold as souvenirs of Canada.

artefacts were the starting point of Juju's design, which also included the politically neutral and widely recognized symbol of Canada, the maple leaf, a particularly apt element of the design because textiles have a long tradition of including floral and plant motifs. The piece was hooked using more than one colour at a time in order to create a pointillist effect with the blend of fabrics and colours. The rug includes beaded details that explicitly refer to the original souvenirs on which the design was based.

Recently, Juju has concentrated on making smaller objects, including hats and bags (see pages 138–139 and 140–141). She continually experiments with colours and shapes, and has evolved a technique for making a piped edging that is stitched into position and then hooked up to. When she makes a hat, the band is made by a hooking, while the top is created from a combination of plain, quilted and stitched fabrics or appliqué. In addition to her roots in Canada, she draws inspiration from the works of Alice Kettle and the Scottish painter John Bellany. In the future she hopes to develop her work by making rag rugs for children by exploiting the textural possibilities of plastic, rubber, velvet and other materials.

PROJECTS

✳

The projects in this section are based on the designs of Margaret Docherty (see pages 116–122), Lizzie Reakes (see pages 124–127), Debbie Siniska (see pages 131–135), Lynne Stein (see pages 136–137), Jenni Stuart-Anderson (see page 130) and Juju Vail (see pages 138–141). *Rag Rug Inspirations* is not just about making rugs, although the techniques used originated in rag rug, or mat, making and this chapter shows how a mixture of techniques, including rag rug making, may be used to produce a variety of artefacts. There are, of course, rugs too: rectangular, circular and star shaped. These are made using hooking, prodding or speed shuttle techniques. In addition, you can learn to create wall hangings, chair pads and mirror frames, or a Christmas stocking for those wishing to make something a little smaller. Rags can be used to make accessories such as an elegant shoulder bag, a brooch or even earrings. A pattern is also given for a smoking cap with a hooked band and a fabric top. It is surprisingly light to wear and very warm.

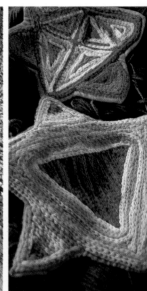

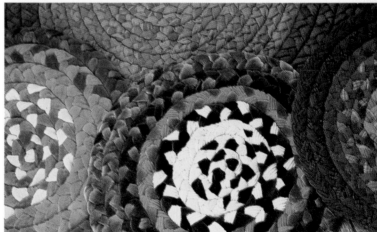

BRAIDED CUSHION PAD

MARGARET DOCHERTY

Depending on the width of each strip of fabric, you can expect to lose about one-third of the length during the plaiting process. As a guide, it takes about 25m (27 yards) of heavy-duty corduroy to make one chair seat. See page 32 for braiding rugs.

1   Cut out strips of fabric, which should be 5–10cm (2–4in) wide to allow for turnings. You may have to join the strips to make them long enough. Do this by stitching along the bias.

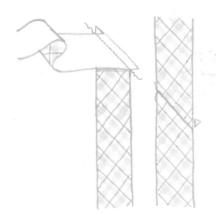

2   Fold the strips with the edges to the centre, then fold again to hide the raw edges. Iron flat or hold with a small running stitch.

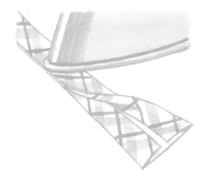

3   Pin three strips together at one end and begin to plait them together. When you need to attach new strips, stitch a new end to the previous one.

4   When the braid is complete, lay it on a flat surface and stitch it together in a spiral large enough to fit on the chair seat. Sew in all raw ends to neaten.

These two braided chair seats were made to fit children's chairs, but the same method can be made to fit chairs of almost any size.
The braids can be stitched together into a variety of shapes.

KNITTED RUG

MARGARET DOCHERTY

The amount of rags required to
make a knitted rug like this
depends on the thickness of the
strips used, the weight of the
fabrics and the tension of the
knitting. When they are worked
with cotton strips, rugs like this
are ideal for bath mats, and they
can even be machine washed.

1 Cut the garment into a single
long strip, if possible cutting in a
spiral. Roll the strip into a ball.

2 Cast on 40 stitches and knit 45
rows. Cast off.

3 Make a border by casting on 8
stitches and knitting until the strip
is long enough to reach all the
way around the square you knitted in step 2. If you want a narrow strip, cast on 6 stitches; if you
want a wider strip, cast on 10
stitches.

4 Lay the square on a flat
surface and overstitch the border
around the outside edge.

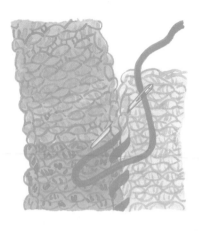

The rug was knitted
on large knitting needles
with strips of cotton dress
fabric. When the central
square had been knitted,
a long strip was added
around the edge to add
textural interest and colour.

HAUSA-SHAPED CHAIN STITCH HANGING

MARGARET DOCHERTY

· The best rags to use are fine knitted ones, particular old T-shirt fabrics. Chain stitch is described on page 35.

1 Cut up the rags into fine strips.

2 Stretch the hessian on a frame. If you are making a small hanging or a Christmas tree decoration an embroidery hoop will be adequate.

3 Use chalk to draw the design on the hessian, allowing space for a border all round, and when you are satisfied with the outlines, go over them with a felt-tipped pen.

The six-pointed star was made by chain stitching T-shirt fabric through a hessian backing. The edges can either be bound with bias binding or overstitched with wool. This is an unusual way of using rags, but the result can be surprisingly delicate.

4 Chain stitch the design by using the hook to make the first hole in the hessian. Hold the fabric strip below the frame and catch the end in the hook. Bring it to the front of the hessian.

5   Insert the hook into the hessian in a new hole, catch the strip and bring it to the front to make a loop.

6   With the hook still in the loop, make a new hole and bring a second loop to the front of the hessian. Pull the second loop through the first one.

7   Repeat the previous step. The process is very similar to embroidered chain stitch. Work the rows close together to form a pattern of concentric circles.

8   When the design is complete, cut the hessian from the frame and trim it, leaving a border of about 2.5cm (1in) all the way round the design.

9   Turn the border to the back and hold it in place with back stitch, close blanket stitch or adhesive, or bind the edge with bias binding before slip stitching it in place. Use a piece of hessian or soft T-shirt fabric as a backing, turning in a neat hem all round to hide all raw edges.

10   Work more than one shape and join them to make a hanging or stitch a loop to the top of the shape if you are making a small decoration.

Here are two alternative ideas. The semicircular mat (above) was worked by chain stitch and the triangles were added around the edge when the basic shape was complete. Also worked in chain stitch (below), this heart-shaped piece, with its handle of twisted wool and cluster of woollen plaits at the centre, could be used to make an evening bag or, worked on a smaller scale, a brooch.

PLAITED AND HOOKED RUG

MARGARET DOCHERTY

4   When the plait spirals are in place, hook around each spiral or swirl using two colours. Make sure that the loops are the same height as the plaits. Continue to fill in the rest of the design in the appropriate colours.

1   Stretch the canvas on the frame, so that it is taut and straight.

2   Draw the design on the front of the hessian in chalk. When you are pleased with the pattern, go over the outlines with a felt-tipped pen.

3   Make several plaits (see page 32) and pin, then stab stitch them in place on the hessian, using a strong thread such as buttonhole thread. Stitch both sides of each plait to the hessian.

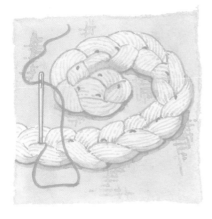

This blue and yellow rug was made by a variety of techniques and a range of materials, including wool and corduroy. The braids were made first and stitched to the hessian backing before the areas around them were filled by hooking.

5 When the design is complete, cut off the rug from the frame, leaving a border of 5cm (2in) all round. Turn the border to the back of the rug and overstitch the edge of the rug with tapestry wool to give a neat finish.

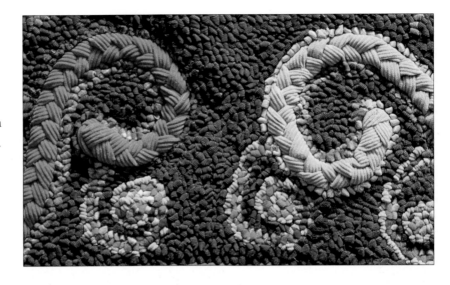

Right: This detail of the rug shows how the braids have been used to create a pattern of waves.

STAR-SHAPED RUG

LIZZIE REAKES

1 Draw the design on paper to the dimensions you want the finished rug to be. Indicate on the paper the colours you intend to use for each area.

2 Trace over the main elements of the design and transfer this to card to create a template. Place the template on the hessian and draw around it, leaving a border of about 10cm (4in) all around. Ensure this guideline is clear.

3 Stretch the hessian taut on a frame, holding it securely in place with staples or drawing pins.

4 Begin to hook, pulling the strips through to the front, while holding the strips under the hessian in your other hand.

5 Continue to hook, forming rows of loop pile and changing colours as wished, until the design is complete. If you wish, cut a pile by shearing across with scissors. Cut out the rug shape, leaving a border 5cm (2in) all around.

6 Remove the rug from the frame and place it face down on a flat, clean surface. Place a piece of hessian over the rug and, feeling

the outline with your hands, carefully draw the shape of the rug on the hessian. (Use your original template if you kept accurately within the outline as you were working.) Cut the hessian to the shape of the finished rug.

Above: The rug was shaped to resemble a star rather than having a star motif hooked into it. When you cut out the backing fabric, remember to leave enough to turn back the edges all round. Lizzie Reakes calls her rug *Green Star*, and she uses it as a wall-hanging.

1 2 3

7 Spread a layer of latex or PVA adhesive over the back of the rug.

Make sure that the surface is completely covered, but do not use too much. Lay the second piece of hessian over the rug and use an iron to bond the two layers together.

8 Carefully snip around the border of the rug, up to the hooking line and backing. Apply a little latex to the snipped pieces and

turn them back neatly on top of the backing. Leave until completely dry before turning the rug over.

◆

STAR-SHAPED BROOCH

LIZZIE REAKES

You can use the same technique to make earrings – simply cut smaller shapes and stick flat earring findings to the back instead of a brooch pin.

1 Draw the star shape on a piece of card to make a template. Cut it out.

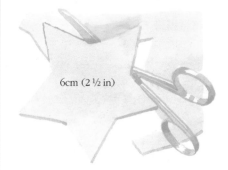

6cm (2 ½ in)

2 Place the template on the square of hessian, centring it on the hessian.

3 Insert the hessian in the embroidery hoop. Make sure that the outline of the star is positioned in the centre of the hoop and that the fabric is held taut and straight.

4 Cut the foil or your chosen material into strips about 1cm (¹/₂ in) wide. Holding the strips under the hoop and beginning in the centre of the star, use your hook to pull the end of a strip of foil through to front of the hessian. Continue to hook the foil strips, working outwards to create an even pile 3 – 4mm (¹/₈ in) high. Check the back of your work from time to time to make sure it is neat.

Right: Star brooches like this are small enough to be hooked on an embroidery frame. The brooch has been backed with felt, to which a small brooch pin can be glued.

5 When you have finished the hooking, check that all the ends are hooked through to the front and trim them neatly.

6 Spread a thin coat of latex or PVA adhesive over the back of the brooch area and leave to dry for about 5 minutes.

7 Take the hessian from the hoop and cut out the star, leaving a border of at least 1cm (¹/₂ in) on all edges.

8 Turn the edges down over the back, snipping the hessian at intervals and pinching the edges to make sure that they are straight and even. Leave to finish drying for about 2 hours.

9 When the latex is completely dry, apply a thin coat of clear all-purpose adhesive to the back of the brooch and place it on a piece of felt. Press it down firmly, then cut around the felt, right up to the hooked star shape.

10 Use strong glue to attach a brooch pin to the centre back of the star. Hold in place for about 30 seconds, then leave to dry before wearing it.

MIRROR FRAMES

LIZZIE REAKES

1 Sketch a shape of your choice on the hessian or trace the design shown here and transfer it to card to make a template. Allow a border of at least 7.5cm (3in) all around the design.

2 Place the hessian in the frame or embroidery hoop, making sure that it is held securely and taut. Using strips in the colours of your choice, begin to hook by bringing one end of the first strip through just beyond the central area.

3 Continue to hook the design, changing colours as you wish until all the areas are filled.

4 Check the back of your work from time to time to make sure that it is neat, and when you have finished check that all the ends of the strips have been hooked through to the front. Trim the ends level with the loops.

5 Remove the hessian from the frame and lay the work face down on a flat surface. Apply a thin layer of latex or adhesive to the reverse, covering the whole of the back of the work, including the blank, central area.

Mirror frames can be hooked on to a hessian backing. Remember to leave a gap
in the centre and to cut this out, leaving a border to turn back and glue to the back of the work.
The mirror is held in a small pocket, and the back was covered with felt, which was stitched in place.

6 Cut around the worked area, leaving a border of about 2cm (1in) all round the design, and cut out the central area, leaving a similar border. Snip the hessian up to the hooking line so that it will lie flat, and fold it to the back, making sure that it lies flat and that all the edges are smooth. Fold back the centre section in the same way. Leave to dry for about 2 hours.

7 Use your card template or use the finished piece to cut around a piece of black felt, adding on a narrow border all round. Apply some clear, all-purpose adhesive to the back of the piece and carefully attach the black felt. Slip stitch the black felt in place all around the frame.

8 Use small, sharp scissors or a craft knife to cut out the central area in the black felt.

9 Using the mirror or the piece of glass as a template, cut a piece of black felt to make a pocket to hold the mirror or glass. Blanket stitch this in position behind the central hole, using strong thread.

10 Finish off by stitching or gluing a hanger to the back of the frame. If you do not have a hanger, use the ring-pull from the top of a drinks can.

Mirror frames can be made in almost any shape you want. Lizzie Reakes often decorates her frames with nodules and spikes, which are sometimes worked in the same colour as the frame and sometimes in contrasting shades.

PINK AND FANCY RUG

ALI RHIND

This prodded rag rug is made from woollen scraps, which are harder wearing and have more 'spring' than other fabrics. Old blankets are particularly good for this kind of rug, and they accept dye very well. See pages 28–30 for prodding.

1 Attach the hessian to the frame, either pinning or stapling it firmly and stretching the hessian until it is taut.

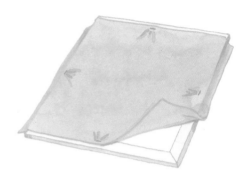

Below: The rug was made by the prodding method, and pieces of woollen blanket were used on a hessian backing.

2 Use a ruler and piece of chalk to draw the design on the back of the hessian (see the outline below). When you are happy with the outlines, go over them with a felt-tipped pen.

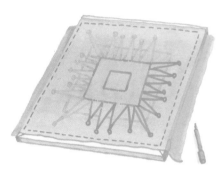

3 Begin to work the design with the colours of your choice, going around the outlines first before filling in the shapes. Use the prodder to push the first scrap half-way into the hessian.

4 Push the other half of the scrap through the next hole in the hessian, making sure that it is level on the other side.

5 Continue to fill the design with the colours of your choice. When the design is complete, take the rug from the frame and trim the hessian to leave a border of about 10cm (4in) all round.

6 Fold the border to the back of the rug, turn in a hem and stitch in place.

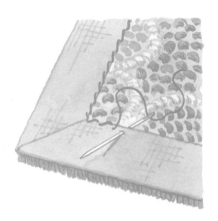

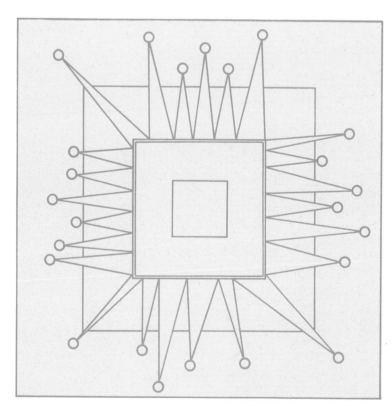

MEL

JENNI STUART ANDERSON

✳ YOU WILL NEED ✳

Hessian

Frame

Strong thread or staples or
pins

Pencil and paper

Felt-tipped pen

Ruler

Selection of woollen sweaters

Upholstery needle and strong
thread

Speed shuttle hook (see pages 21
and 26 for hooking)

1 Fix the hessian to your frame, using strong thread, staples or pins. Make sure that the hessian is as taut as possible and that it is absolutely straight.

2 Using the image of a dog from a photograph or book, simplify the outlines and transfer them to the back of the hessian. Because you will be working from the back, make sure that any details are reversed – your outlines will be a mirror-image of the finished rug. If you find it difficult to draw an accurate representation, enlarge the photograph in a photocopier and trace the outline and some details so that you can transfer the lines to the hessian by means of a transfer pencil or carbon paper.

3 Use a long ruler and a felt-tipped pen to indicate the perimeter of the rug on the hessian.

4 Take a selection of old woollen sweaters in a variety of colours, wash them and cut off all the seams. Cut the material into 1cm (³/8 in) strips.

5 Work the animal image first. Begin by going around the outline, and then fill in the same colour areas with parallel rows. Add the spots and facial details last.

6 Hook the outside border, then complete the background with your chosen colours.

7 Cut the work from the frame, leaving a hessian border about 5cm (2in) wide all round. Turn in the border as a hem on the back of the rug, and stitch it in place, using an upholstery needle and a strong thread (buttonhole thread is ideal).

Below: Dogs have always been favourite subjects of rag rug makers, and Jenni Stuart-Anderson's *Mel* continues this tradition. Note how the top of the head and the tip of the tail and front paw just break into the frame of the rug.

JEWEL MOON DOOR ARCH

DEBBIE SINISKA

To make a rag rug to fit over a door arch, carefully measure the door and transfer the dimensions to a piece of hessian. Remember to allow extra for turning back and for hangers so that a baton can be used to support the arch above the door.

1 Set up the frame and attach the hessian to it, using strong thread to tie it to the edges. Keep the tension of the hessian as tight as you can.

2 Chalk the design on the reverse of the hessian, because you will be working from the back. When you are satisfied with it, go over the outlines with a felt-tipped pen or marker so that you can see the lines clearly.

3 Begin at one edge of the hessian and work around the perimeter of the design.

4 Fill in the shapes of the design with your chosen colours, checking the front of your work from time to time and neatening it as necessary.

5 When you have completely filled in the design, take the work off the frame by unfastening the

131

threads holding the hessian. Lay the piece face down on a flat surface.

6 Make a backing by cutting a piece of hessian to the exact measurement of the door arch.

Stitch or glue this backing down on the back of the work.

7 Trim off the edges of the front part of the design, leaving a border of about 10cm (4in) all round.

Snip all along the outside edge up the hook line, then turn them neatly over to the back so that they overlap the backing hessian, securing them in place with latex or adhesive.

FLYING HEART DOOR MAT

DEBBIE SINISKA

This lively design is an original variation on the theme of a heart with wings. The bright pink heart stands out from the calmer background, but the wings appear to be swaying in the wind.

*2 pieces of hessian,
  approximately 75 x 50 cm
  (30 x 20 in) or 1 side of
  a peanut sack*
Frame
Chalk

Felt-tipped pen or Magic Marker
*Selection of fabrics, cut into
  strips about 1cm (¹/₂ in) wide*
Speed shuttle hook (see page 21)
Scissors
Needle and strong thread

Above: Detail of *Flying Heart Door Mat*

1 Set up the frame and attach one of the pieces of hessian to it, using strong thread to tie it to the edges. Keep the tension of the hessian as tight as you can.

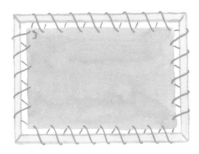

2 Chalk the design on the reverse of the hessian, because you will be working from the back. When you are satisfied with it, go over the outlines with a felt-tipped pen or marker so that you can see the lines clearly.

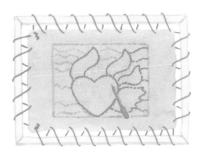

3 Begin at one edge of the hessian and work around the perimeter of the design.

4 Fill in the shapes of the design with your chosen colours, checking the front of your work from time to time and neatening it as necessary.

5 When you have completely filled in the design, take the work off the frame by unfastening the threads holding the hessian. Lay the rug face up on a flat surface. Trim the edges of the hessian, leaving a border of about 10cm (4in) all round.

6 Roll this allowance neatly up on the right side and secure it by stitching it down as close as possible to the edge of the hooking to form a piping. Mitre the angles of the corners.

7 Take the second piece of hessian and trim it to the exact dimensions of the finished rug. Stitch it carefully to the back of the rug, turning under the raw edges as you work.

PINK SUN BANNER

DEBBIE SINISKA

The design for this banner could be used as a rug or as a wall-hanging. It has an unusual shape, and when you are finishing it off, you must take care that the hessian is not visible from the front. You may find it easier to stitch down the seam allowance on the back, because when you use glue you have to work much more quickly.

1 Set up the frame and attach one of the pieces of hessian to it, using strong thread to tie it to the edges. Keep the tension of the hessian as tight as you can.

2 Chalk the design on the reverse of the hessian, because you will be working from the back. When you are satisfied with it, go over the outlines with a felt-tipped pen or marker so that you can see the lines clearly.

3 Select your colours and cut them into strips. Although they should be about 1cm (1/2 in) wide, if you are using very thick fabric make them slightly wider; if you are using especially fine fabric make them narrower. Introduce interest and texture to the depth of the pile by cutting the materials to different widths.

4 Begin at one edge of the hessian and work around the perimeter of the design.

5 Fill in the shapes of the design with your chosen colours, checking the front of your work from time to time and neatening it as necessary.

6 When you have completely filled in the design, take the work off the frame by unfastening the threads holding the hessian. Lay the banner face down on a flat surface.

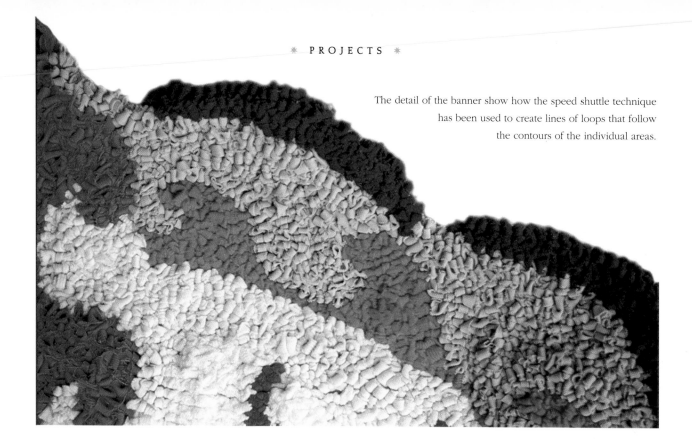

The detail of the banner show how the speed shuttle technique has been used to create lines of loops that follow the contours of the individual areas.

7 Trim all the edges, leaving a border of 5cm (2in) on all edges except for the scalloped border.

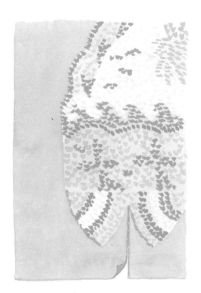

Here, cut straight down between each scallop, trim the hessian and cut evenly spaced tabs up to the hooking line.

8 Turn the border to the back and use latex or a rubber-based adhesive to hold it down. Pay particular attention to the indentations and curves of the scallops, making sure that the curves are smooth and neat.

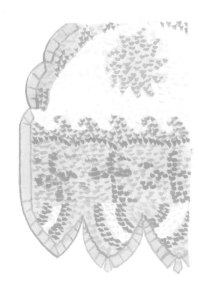

9 Cover the turned-down edge with cotton binding tape, using latex or adhesive to secure the tape and pressing it down smoothly with a small decorator's roller. Mitre the binding at the corners where necessary.

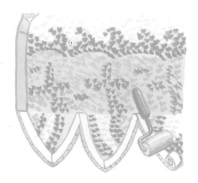

10 Use lengths of cotton binding to make loops for hanging the banner and stab stitch them to the back of the work, positioning them about 10cm (4in) down from the top edge.

CHRISTMAS STOCKING

LYNNE STEIN

1 Draw the shape of the Christmas stocking, using the outline on page 137 as a guide. Cut out the shape on thin card to use as a template.

2 Draw around the template on the hessian, adding a design of your choice or following the pattern shown in the photograph.

3 Attach the hessian to the frame so that it is taut and straight, then use strips of fabrics to hook the pattern in the boot shape.

Above: A special Christmas stocking would make a wonderful gift, and the design can be easily modified to make a front and back. You can either simply turn in the edges all round or make a drop-in lining to disguise the raw edges.

4 Take the hessian from the frame and cut out the boot, adding a border of 5cm (2in) all round. Snip the border to the hooking line and turn it back, gluing or stitching it in place.

5 Cut out the same shape, adding on the seam allowance, for the back of the stocking from another piece of hessian or a piece of backing fabric. Neaten the top edge by turning down a hem and stitching it in place with small running stitches.

6 Turning in the seam allowance as you work, stitch the back of the stocking to the hooked front.

7 Stitch silk piping or cord around the edge of the stocking to cover the side seam. Make a loop at the top edge so that you can hang up the stocking, then make a tassel by teasing out the threads at the end of the cord and wrapping them with gold thread.

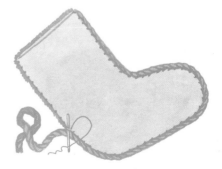

SMOKING CAP

JUJU VAIL

1 Make the side piece of the hat by measuring the circumference of the head and adding 5cm (2in). Draw a rectangle on a piece of hessian that is the length of the side piece (including allowance) by 6cm (2½ in) deep. Cut out the rectangle.

2 Rather than using traditional piping cord, make you own piping. You will need two strips, each the length of the head circumference plus 9cm (3½ in) and 5.5cm (2¼ in) deep. Cut out the two rectangles on the bias of your chosen fabric. Cut two strips of blanket, each the length of the piping fabric but 5cm (2in) deep.

3 Place one piece of the piping fabric along the top edge of the hessian side band so that it overlaps each side equally and the top edges align. Pin then stitch in place. Place the second piece of piping fabric along the bottom edge of the hessian, aligning the bottom edges and centring the piping fabric over the hessian. Pin and stitch in place.

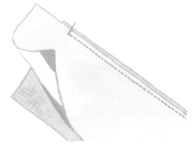

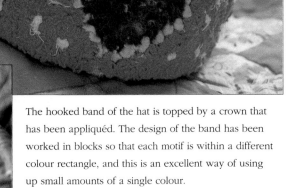

The hooked band of the hat is topped by a crown that has been appliquéd. The design of the band has been worked in blocks so that each motif is within a different colour rectangle, and this is an excellent way of using up small amounts of a single colour.

4 Place the blanket strips or piping cord on the piping fabric at the top of the hessian. Fold over the piping fabric to enclose the blanket or cord and stitch in place, sewing along the first row of stitches. Repeat along the bottom edge.

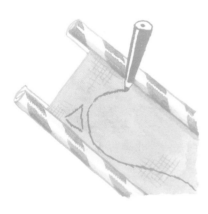

5 Place the hessian on a flat surface and draw on your design. Make sure that there is a plain or unimportant section of the design at the ends of the hessian rectangle so that you can adjust the fit as necessary without spoiling the appearance of the pattern.

6 Hook the design into the hessian, working right up to the piping and to the ends of the hessian so that no backing fabric is visible.

7 Apply a coat of latex or rubber-based adhesive all over the back of the completed design. Leave to dry. Apply latex or adhesive to the back of the seam allowance of the piping fabric and press it down against the back of the hooked design so that the piping is erect along the top and bottom edges.

8 With the right sides together, join the two short ends to create the back seam. Stitch this by hand using an upholstery needle and strong thread. If the hessian shows through, stitch the hook or hooks in place to cover it. Fold in the raw edges of the blanket or piping cord at the seam and slip stitch to join the folded edges.

9 Make the crown of the hat by drawing a circle on the fabric that is 4cm (1½ in) greater than the diameter of the side piece so that there is a seam allowance of 2cm (about 1in) all round.

The sides of the smoking cap are hooked from a variety of materials, and the motifs are outlined in strips of foil paper to emphasize the design.

10 With the side piece inside out and, with right sides facing, pin the circle of fabric you have cut for the crown in place, easing it to fit around the curves. Stitch in place by hand, using slip stitch.

11 Cut a rectangle and a circle from the lining fabric. These should be slightly smaller than the hessian band and crown – approximately 2cm (1in) less on all dimensions. Stitch the back seam of the band, adjusting it to fit inside the hat, then pin and stitch the crown lining to the band lining. Turn in and press the bottom raw edge before inserting the lining in the hat. Slip stitch in place around the bottom so that all raw edges are hidden.

EVENING BAG

JUJU VAIL

✳ YOU WILL NEED ✳

Tape measure, paper and pencil

Scissors

Felt-tipped pen

Hessian

Material for piping and old blanket or piping cord

Hook (see page 26 for hooking)

Selection of rags

Latex or rubber-based adhesive

Material for the strap, lining and sides

Needle and thread

Zip

2 D-loops

1 Transfer the outline of the pattern for the front, base and back to the front of the hessian. Cut out the hessian piece, leaving a small seam allowance all round.

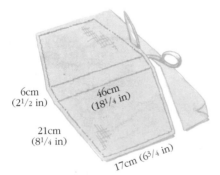

6cm (2¹/₂ in)

46cm (18¹/₄ in)

21cm (8¹/₄ in)

17cm (6³/₄ in)

2 Make the piping cord (see page 140). You will need two lengths, each about 19cm (7in) long.

3 Sew the cord to the front of the hessian so that there is a small overlap at each end for the turnings.

4 Hook the design on the hessian, using a variety of fabrics. The bag shown in the photograph has a motif surrounded by a border on the front and back, or you could follow the design shown in the illustration and separate the motifs on the front and back by working a chequered section along the base. Hook right up to the piped edges.

5 Apply latex or adhesive to the seam allowance of the piping and press it down to the back of the bag so that the piping is erect.

6 Cut out two gusset pieces from material, with a seam allowance of about 2.5cm (1in), and, with right sides facing, pin one side to the front of the bag. Align the widest portion of the gusset with the base of the bag, then align the other side of the gusset with one side of the back of the bag. Repeat at the other side. Stitch in place as shown.

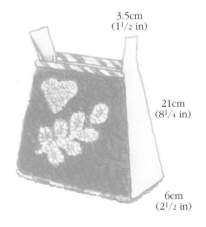

3.5cm (1¹/₂ in)

21cm (8¹/₄ in)

6cm (2¹/₂ in)

7 Turn the bag the right way out and stitch the zip fastener in place across the top opening.

8 Cut pieces for the lining, including the two gussets, but making all pieces 2cm (about 1in) smaller in all directions than the bag. Stitch the lining gusset pieces to the front/back lining piece, then insert the lining into the bag so that wrong sides are facing. Turn under the raw edges of the top of the lining and slip stitch in place along the piping line.

9 Attach D-rings to the top of the gusset. Use a length of leather or cord or make a fabric strap and stitch this securely through the D-rings.

The front (*above*) and back (*below*) of the shoulder bag were worked on one piece of hessian and fabric gussets were added to the sides when the design had been hooked. The top of the bag has been edged with piping, and it could be lined with a drop-in lining to hide the raw edges. Add a zip fastener or, if you prefer, a large press-stud to close the bag.

141

FURTHER READING

Artists as Rug Makers (catalogue), Boveridge Press, 26 Fernshaw Road, London SW10, 1994

Betterton, Sheila, *Rugs*, American Museum in Britain, 1981

Boswell, Thom (editor), *The Rug Hook Book*, Sterling Publishing Co. Inc., New York, 1992 (paperback edition 1994)

Crouse, Gloria E., *Hooking Rugs: New Materials, New Techniques*, Taunton Press, Newtown, Connecticut, 1990

Davies, Ann, *Rag Rugs*, Letts Contemporary Crafts, London, 1992

Davies, Ann, and Tennant, Emma, *Hooked Rugs*, Museum Quilts, London, 1995

Hinchcliffe, John, *Rugs from Rags*, 1977

Kent, William Winthrop, *The Hooked Rug*, New York, 1937 (reprinted by Gale Research, Detroit, 1971)

Meany, Janet, and Pfaff, Paul, *Rag Rug Handbook*, Dos Tejedoras Fiber Arts Publications, Saint Paul, Minneapolis, 1988

Moshimer, Joan, *The Complete Rug Hooker*, New York Graphic Society, Boston, 1975; Dover Publications, London, 1975

Rag Rugs (Needlecrafts, no. 10), Search Press, London, 1980

Ragtime Rugs and Wall Hangings: An Exhibition of Rag Rugs Old and New (catalogue), Shipley Art Gallery, Consort Road, Gateshead, 1988

Sturges, Norma M., *The Braided Rug Book: Creating Your Own Folk Art*, Lark Books, 1995

Tennant, Emma, *Rag Rugs of England and America*, Walker Books, London, 1992

PICTURE CREDITS

ARTISTS AND STOCKISTS

The artists and rug makers whose work is featured in this book have kindly agreed that their addresses be included. Many of them give lectures and run courses or hold workshops on rug making, supply rug making equipment and undertake commissions, both private and public. Write to them, enclosing a large stamped, addressed envelope, for further details. International reply coupons, available from post offices, should be sent to overseas makers.

ARTISTS

Prue Bramwell-Davis
40 Arminger Road
London W12 7BB

Barbara Carroll
Woolley Fox
61 Old Lincoln Highway
East Ligonier
PA 15658
USA

Louisa Creed
27 Norfolk Street
York YO2 1JY

Ann Davies
1 Wingrad House
Jubilee Street
London E1 3JB

Margaret Docherty
Ruskin Mill Workshops
Old Bristol Road
Nailsworth
Gloucestershire GL6 0LA

Nancy Edell
R.R.1 Bayswater
Hubbards
Nova Scotia
Canada B0J IT0

Sarah Flatman
Higher Trickies Farm House
Morebath
Tiverton
Devon EX16 9AL

Ben Hall
Flat 2
56 Glenwood Road
London SE6 4NF

Nicky Hessenberg
60 Westbourne Park Villas
London W2 5EB

Liz Kitching
Hill Cottage
Walton
Brampton
Cumbria CA8 2EA

Susan Lindsay
44 ½ Victoria Park Avenue
Toronto
Ontario
Canada M4E 3R9

Lu Mason
86 Lindley Street
York YO2 4JS

Alison Morton
Eagles Yard
Machynlleth
Powys
Wales

Lizzie Reakes
68 Oaklands Road
Hanwell
Ealing
London W7 2DU

Ali Rhind Design Studio
Ouseburn Warehouse
36 Lime Street
Newcastle upon Tyne NE1 2PN
(For slides of Ali Rhind's work contact: Brian Wade, The Bungalow, Woodhorn Village, Ashington, Northumberland NE63 9YA or Nigel Shuttleworth, Yew House, Allery Banks, Morpeth, Northumberland NE61 2SW)

Debbie Siniska
Glyndale
St Mary's Lane
Ticehurst
East Sussex TN5 7AX

Lynne Stein
4 Oakfield Court
Grey Road
Altrincham
Cheshire WA14 4BX

Jenni Stuart-Anderson
Leysters
The Birches, Middleton on the Hill
Herefordshire HR6 0HZ

Amanda Townend
150 Barlow Moor Road
West Didsbury
Manchester M20 2UT

Carmel Treanor
Eshacrin
New Inn Road
Hinxworth
Baldock,
Herts SG7 5HE

Juju Vail
6 Alconbury Road
London E5 8RH

STOCKISTS

Australia and New Zealand
E. & F. Good
31 Landsdowne Terrace
Walkerville
SA 5081, Australia

D.M.C. Needlecrafts
PO Box 317
Earlwood
NSW 2206, Australia

Auckland Folk Art Centre
591 Remuera Road
Remuera
Auckland, New Zealand

Canada
Rittermere-Hurst-Field
45 Tyler Street
Box 487
Aurora, Ontario L4G 3L6
(designs and supplies; catalogue $6.00)

UK
Russell & Chapple
23 Monmouth Street
London WC2H 9DD

Fred Aldous
37 Lever Street, Manchester M60 1UX
tel: 0161 236 2477; fax: 0161236 6075
(mail order rug equipment)

USA
Forestheart Studio
21 South Carroll Street
Frederick, MD 21701
(linen backing material, dyes, cutters, frames, wool, hooks)

INDEX